How GOD Will Restore Your Marriage

There's Healing After Broken Vows!

A Book for MEN

Erin Thiele

NarrowRoad Publishing House

How GOD Will Restore Your Marriage
There's Healing After Broken Vows

By Erin Thiele

Published by:
NarrowRoad Publishing House
POB 830
Ozark, MO 65721 U.S.A.

The materials from Restore Ministries were written for the sole purpose of encouraging women and men. For more information, visit us at:

www.NRPH.org
www.RestoreMinistries.net
www.RMIEW.com
www.EncouragingMEN.org

Unless otherwise indicated, most Scripture verses are taken from the New American Standard Bible (NASB). Scripture quotations marked KJV are taken from the King James Version of the Bible, and Scripture quotations marked NIV are taken from the New International Version. Our ministry is not partial to any particular version of the Bible but love them all for the purpose of helping everyone in every denomination.

Cover Design by Dallas Thiele

First Printing 1996
Second Printing 1997, revised
Third Printing 1999, completely revised
Fourth Printing 2003, completely revised
Fifth Printing 2004, completely revised

ISBN: 1-931800-03-0
ISBN 13: 978-1-931800-03-7
LOC: 2015910009

Contents

Chapter 1

Peace From God

"...to all who are beloved of God...
Grace to you and peace from God
our Father and the Lord Jesus Christ"
Romans 1:7

Dear Beloved Brother in Christ,

It is not by chance that you are holding this book in your hands; it is by Divine Providence. God has heard your cry for help and He has come to rescue you. The pages that follow will guide you when others tell you that your situation is completely hopeless.

What He is asking you to do will not be easy but if you want a miracle in your life, it can happen. If you want a testimony of the faithfulness of God to share with others, it will happen. If you really want God to restore a marriage that is hopeless, then read on. God will restore your marriage as He did mine.

The Bible says "the eyes of the Lord move to and fro throughout the earth that He may strongly support those whose heart is completely His." 2Chr. 16:9. He has been looking for you, to help you. Are you ready?

You will need zealous obedience. You must enter "by the narrow gate; and the way is narrow that leads to life, and few are those who find it. For the gate is wide, and the way is broad that leads to destruction, and many are those who enter by it." Matt. 7:14. It is your choice whether to follow His narrow way now or turn back.

This is the time to choose. "I call heaven and earth to witness against you today, that I have set before you life and death, the blessing and the curse. So choose life in order that you may live, you and your descendants, by loving the Lord your God, by obeying His voice, and by holding fast to Him; for this is yor life and the length of your days." Deut. 30:19-20.

If you are still reading and have not thrown this book away, then you have chosen to go on. We rejoice with you as we think of the glorious resurrection of your marriage and family that awaits you. We pray blessings upon each and every one of you. We glory that some day we will meet either on this side or the other side of "heaven" where there are no more tears or pain.

Dear brother in Christ Jesus, God will restore your marriage: you have **His** Word on it. "And Jesus answered and said to them, 'Truly I say to you, if you have faith, and do not doubt, you shall not only do what was done…but even if you say to this mountain, "Be taken up and cast into the sea," it shall happen.'" Matt. 21:21.

Since you are reading this book, we assume that you are in a crisis in your life because of your marriage. Has your wife left you? Have you left or asked your wife to leave? Perhaps you have gotten this book before either of you has taken this drastic step of leaving. Even if divorce has been spoken of during an argument, or divorce papers have been filed, or a divorce has gone through, you must believe that "All things (**can**) work together for good to those who love God and are called according to *His* **purpose**." Rom. 8:28.

As you go through personal trials in your troubled marriage, if you really want things to work out for good, you must first love God and really want **His** purpose for your life.

Right now His purpose is for you to draw closer to Him, to let Him transform you more closely into His image. And take courage, for God has said, "I will never leave you, nor forsake you." Hebr. 13:5. God has not left your side: "Yea though I walk through the valley of the shadow of death, I will fear no evil, for *Thou art with me*." Psalm 23:4.

I'm sure that the "valley of the shadow of death" describes how you feel about your situation, but God has
allowed this for *your* **good**.

Only afterwards will you shine forth as gold. "In this you greatly rejoice, even though for a little while, if necessary, you have been distressed by various trials, that the proof of your faith, being more precious than gold (which is perishable) even though tested by fire, may be found to result in praise, glory and honor." 1Pet. 1:7.

The most important thing for you to do right now is "be still and know that I am God." Ps. 46:10. (This is covered in more depth in the men's **Take Courage** series.) Then follow God's way. Make sure that everything that you do or say follows the Scriptures; be sure that it follows the Bible consistently.

God has no desire for your marriage to be over. Remember that Jesus Himself said, "a man shall leave his mother and father and cleave to his wife and the two shall become one flesh. Consequently, they are no longer two but one flesh. What God has joined together let no man separate." Matt. 19:5. Also, " 'I hate divorce,' says the Lord God of Israel. 'So take heed to your spirit.'" Mal. 2:16.

Satan is the one who wants your marriage destroyed, not the Lord, not God. Remember that "The thief (the devil) comes to steal, to kill and destroy; I came that (you) might have life, and might have it abundantly." John 10:10. Don't believe the devil's lies but "take **every** thought captive." 2Cor. 10:5.

Don't allow him to steal your wife. Don't allow him to destroy your family, your life, and your children and steal your future. Believe me and believe others who can tell you from experience that divorce will destroy children and steal your children's future as well as your own.

Follow God's way instead to find true peace in the midst of your crisis. " 'For the mountains may be removed and the hills may shake, but My lovingkindness will not be removed from you, and My covenant of peace will not be shaken,' says the LORD who has compassion on you." Isa. 54:10.

Pore over the Bible, letting Him "wash you with the water of the Word." Eph. 5:26. Pray and believe what Scripture says, not what you see: "Faith is the assurance of things hoped for, the conviction of things **not seen**." Hebr. 11:1. "And without faith it is impossible to please (God)." Hebr. 11:6.

No one but God knows exactly what you are going through or the answers you need right now. If you pray (simply talk to God) and listen to Him (read His Word, the Bible), He can lead you to the victory that He has for you. Don't choose to follow what others may say, those of the world, friends in the church, pastors, or any counselor who tells you something he has heard or read. If you are praying and reading God's Word, God will speak to you first, in your heart or during your Bible reading; then someone will confirm the direction in which **He** is guiding you, which will be consistent with His Word!

Too many people, Christian or not, tell you things that sound good and feel good in the flesh. But if it doesn't follow Scripture, **it is wrong**! You will be on sinking sand. "Blessed is the man who does not walk in the counsel of the wicked." Ps. 1:1. When it is of God, it usually sounds crazy (like believing for your marriage when others say "get out"!) and it always needs the help of the Holy Spirit to carry it out.

Don't act impulsively or be quick to move. God usually says, "Wait!" Many times during the wait, He changes the situation. God said that He is the "Wonderful and Mighty Counselor." Isa. 9:6. Don't you want the best? Wouldn't you want a counselor who knows the future? One who can actually turn the heart of your wife? There is only One who can show you the right direction. Trust Him and Him alone! There are actually MORE broken marriages in the church than there are in the world, so don't follow any Christian, Christian counselor, or pastor who gives the world's advice instead of God's.

Sadly, Christian marriage counselors destroy too many Christian marriages. They get you and your wife to talk about the past and to say things that should never be said. Cruel statements are lies of the devil or fleshly feelings. Then after the counselor listens to what he/she has prompted you to say, he/she will tell you that your situation is hopeless!

If someone (including your spouse) has told you that your situation is hopeless, then start to praise the Lord. Hopeless situations are exactly where the Lord chooses to show His power! "With men this is impossible but **with God** ALL things are possible!" Matt. 19:26.

Work with God. And don't believe that without your wife's help or cooperation your marriage can't be saved or improved. Our ministry was founded by and for those who are the only partner seeking marriage restoration! All that is needed is your heart and the Lord's strength. "For the eyes of the Lord run to and fro throughout the whole earth that He may support those whose heart is completely His." 2Chr. 16:9.

Take the privilege of being "counseled" by the Best Counselor. The truth is that no two situations are exactly alike; nevertheless, His Word applies to all. "Blessed be the God and Father of our Lord Jesus Christ, the Father of mercies and God of all comfort; who comforts us in all our affliction so that we may be able to comfort those who are in any affliction with the comfort with which we ourselves are comforted by God." 2Cor. 1:3-4.

Search His Word, after you have prayed. "Ask and it shall be given to you; seek and you shall find." Matt. 7:7. "But if any of you lacks wisdom, let him ask of God, who gives to all men generously and without reproach, and it will be given to him. But let him ask in faith without any doubting, for the one who doubts is like the surf of the sea driven and tossed by the wind. For let not that man expect that he will receive anything from the Lord, being a double-minded man, unstable in all his ways." Jas. 1:5.

You must have faith! And where do you get faith? From God! Ask Him for faith since "All good things come from above." Jas. 1:17.

God's Word, His Principles

Beloved, whether you know the Bible well or you have never even read it before, the Bible ALONE must be your guide to restore your marriage. The book that you are reading consists of all the verses that the Lord used to guide others, who now have restored marriages, through the fires of trial to restoration.

The Lord will begin to show you, through the Scriptures in this book, how you may have violated principles of marriage, and He will also show you other sins that you are unaware of or have never dealt with (by repenting of them). All of these sins and violations have led to the destruction of your marriage.

It is the same with ALL who find their marriages in shambles or completely destroyed. You will soon find, if you are not aware of it yet, that it is NOT just your wife who violated God's principles by leaving you, being unfaithful or filing for divorce. You will find, as did others who now have restored marriages, that you have done much to contribute to the destruction of your marriage. This understanding will be the turning point as you accept and look at your sins, not your wife's.

The wisdom that you will learn from reading and rereading the verses of Scripture that the Lord has for you in this book will help you to understand what the Bible really is and what you need it to be in your life – your guide.

The Bible is filled with the spiritual laws of His creation. When God created the world, He not only made it with physical laws, like the law of gravity, but He also created it with spiritual laws. Just as violating the physical law of gravity will result in you stumbling or an object falling, so will violating the principles in Scripture regarding marriage result in your marriage falling.

Another amazing discovery is that the ways of the world are almost always opposite the ways of God and His Word. The way you have been dealing with your wife's leaving you, her unfaithfulness or the divorce papers she served you, more than likely is the same way that anyone in the world would have dealt with them. What you will find in this book is that this is the exact OPPOSITE of the way that God intended trials to be dealt with in order to bring victory. "This is the victory that has overcome the world — our faith." 1John 5:4.

When you choose to follow God's way, which is the opposite of the way everyone else is doing it or telling you to do it, then you will start to see your marriage turn around. The ways of the world ALWAYS result in destruction, but the ways of God ALWAYS bring about healing and restoration. "For the one who sows to his own flesh shall from the flesh reap corruption, but the one who sows to the Spirit shall from the Spirit reap eternal life." Gal. 6:8.

We have put together a quick reference in this chapter to help you to IMMEDIATELY get your marriage out of crisis. These principles, if followed to the letter with a sincere and humble heart, will result in an immediate or future restoration of your marriage. God's Word GUARANTEES it!!

The more a man follows these principles, the more restoration he will see as a direct result of his obedience. Those who stay in crisis, or who never see their marriages restored, are those who refuse to believe and obey the spiritual laws of God or erroneously believe that they are above the laws of God.

If you are one of those who believe strongly that you are not "under the law" and are therefore free to violate God's laws, "may it never be!"

"What then? Shall we sin because we are not under law but under grace? **May it never be!**" Rom. 6:15.

"Do we then nullify the Law through faith? **May it never be!** On the contrary, we establish the Law." Rom. 3:31.

"**May it never be!** How shall we who died to sin still live in it?" Rom. 6:2.

Those who understood the law of gravity learned to rise above it, which resulted in man being able to fly. The Christian who studies the Word of God will rise above the world and astonish the unbeliever who will then seek God. However, a person who believes that he is above the law of gravity, and violates that law by jumping out of a plane without a parachute, will fall to his death. This is why so many Christians live lives full of destruction.

Believe and Obey

If you are like many men who want to restore their marriages, you must not only believe that God can restore your marriage, but you must also obey His Word. Are you desperate – desperate to follow God's Word no matter what it costs? No matter how much it hurts? The question you must ask yourself is "How important is saving my marriage, my family, my future?"

Receive anything. If you don't obey God with zealous obedience, you should expect nothing from Him because you are double-minded. "For let not that man expect that he will **receive anything** from the Lord, being a double-minded man, unstable in all his ways." Jas. 1:7-8. "I hate those who are double-minded, but I love Thy law." Ps. 119:113.

Faith by my works. If you say you have the faith to trust God for your marriage, then "act" on it. "What *use is it*, my brethren, if a man says he has faith, but he has no works? Can that faith save him?... But someone may well say, 'You have faith, and I have works; show me your faith without the works, and I will show you my faith **by my works.**' " Jas. 2:14, 18. There are so many testimonies of those who chose to "believe" instead of obeying. Every one of them is still "believing" for his marriage, but not ONE is restored!

Tear it out, and throw it from you. Again, how important is your desire to have a restored marriage? Are you desperate enough to do "whatever it takes" to save it? If you don't believe God calls us to that kind of obedience, look at what Jesus said in Matt. 5:29-30.

"And if your right eye makes you stumble, **tear it out, and throw it from you**; for it is better for you that one of the parts of your body perish, than for your whole body to be thrown into hell. And if your right hand makes you stumble, cut it off, and throw it from you; for it is better for you that one of the parts of your body perish, than for your whole body to go into hell."

Through the entire chapter of Matthew 5, Jesus calls us to a higher obedience than what had been written in the Old Testament. Read it to motivate yourself to obey to the point of looking like a fanatic. If what you are doing right now does not seem crazy to others, you need to become more radical in your commitment to your marriage, because that's what it takes!

We all must be like Peter in our obedience. Each time he was asked to do something, like allowing Jesus to wash his feet, he went overboard! He even went overboard when Jesus asked him to get out of the boat. He was the only one who followed Jesus with such a zealous commitment. Even so, Jesus rebuked Peter for his little faith. Are you lukewarm? "So **because you are lukewarm**, and neither hot nor cold, I will spit you out of My mouth." Rev. 3:16.

Trust and believe that God is able and wants to restore and rebuild you, your marriage, and your family. God does not have any other person out there for you, nor does He think you've picked the wrong person. "...if any man be above reproach, **the husband of ONE wife**, having children who believe, not accused of dissipation or rebellion." Titus 1:6.

If you are thinking about remarriage, you should know this; that second marriage has **less than** a 20% chance of survival! You would have an 8 out of 10 chance of going through another painful divorce! Then it's on to numbers three and four. Stop now at whatever number you are on. There is a better way!

Instead, "Be strong, and let your heart take courage, all you who hope in the Lord." Ps. 27:14, Ps. 31:24, Isa. 35:4. "O give us help against the adversary, for deliverance by man is in vain. Through God we shall do valiantly, and it is He who will tread down our adversaries." Ps. 60:11, Ps. 108:12. (Please read chapter 11, "Cleave to His Wife" for more knowledge.)

Don't run to others about your situation; talk to God; search His Word for your answer. "Seek and you shall find." Matt. 7:7, Luke 11:9. "He is the Mighty Counselor." Isa. 9:6. "Do not walk in the counsel of the ungodly." Ps. 1:1. Don't tell others about your situation: "May a slanderer not be established in the earth." Ps. 140:11.

Also, "by your words you will be justified and by your words you will be condemned." Matt. 12:37. "A tale-bearer separates intimate friends." Prov. 16:28, Prov. 17:9. (See Chapter 4, "Thrusts of a Sword" for more knowledge on the destruction our tongues can cause. Such knowledge is not optional but essential: "For My people perish for a lack of knowledge." Hos. 4:6.)

Ask God for a **male** prayer partner who will believe God with you for your marriage. We encourage you to join our Restoration Fellowship if you have an Internet connection. We will pair you up with an Encouragement Partner who will encourage you, pray for you and help you stay accountable to the principles for restoring your marriage.

Stay away from singles groups!! You do NOT belong there if you have a desire to restore your marriage! Stay away from "support groups" that are usually nothing more than "pity parties." If you want a restored marriage, don't attend a divorce recovery group that will encourage you to move on. You have to choose now whether you want hope or closure with your marriage.

Instead of joining a group in your church or community, we strongly suggest that you pray about joining our fellowship where you will be given a partner. For more information, visit our website www.MarriageHelpOnLine.com.

Stop ALL arguing or verbal struggling with your wife! This one principle will be a deciding factor as to whether your marriage will be restored. There are so many Scriptures on this topic, pages and pages we could type out for you. Here are just a few: "**Agree** with your adversary *quickly!*" Matt. 5:25, KJV. "A gentle answer turns away wrath, but harsh words stir up anger." Prov. 15:1. "The beginning of strife is like letting out of water, so abandon the quarrel before it breaks out." Prov. 17:14. "Even a fool is considered wise when keeping silent." Prov. 17:28.

"Keeping away from strife is an honor for a man. But any **fool** will quarrel." Prov. 20:3. And, "He who separates himself seeks his own desire, he quarrels against all sound wisdom." Prov. 18:1. Are you an angry man? (See Chapter 3, "The Angry Man" and Chapter 9, "Weapons of Our Warfare" for more knowledge.)

Remove the hate or hurt; then try to look lovingly into your wife's eyes. "They looked to Him and were radiant, and their faces shall never be ashamed." Ps. 34:5. "And whoever exalts himself shall be humbled; and whoever humbles himself shall be exalted." Matt. 23:12, Luke 14:11, Luke 18:14. Peter asked how many times he should forgive his brother who sinned against him. "Seven times?" he suggested. But Jesus replied, "I do not say to you, up to seven times, but up to seventy times seven." That's 490 times! (Matt. 18:22) Have you decided to *not* **forgive** your wife (or the man she is involved with) for what she (or he) has done to you or to your children? The lack of forgiveness is very dangerous to you and the future of your marriage. (For more knowledge read Chapter 6, "Blessed Are the Meek" under the section "Forgiveness.") If you are having trouble forgiving, get our testimony tape. It is a powerful example of how God will "give you" the forgiveness your wife desperately needs as you yield to Him!

You must begin to see your wife as God sees her. Pray for your wife. You need to first forgive her and any who are involved with her (friends, family, co-workers and even the other man). (Again, see Chapter 6, "Blessed Are the Meek" under the section "Forgiveness" about the dangers of **not** forgiving.) Then you will be ready to pray for the woman God wants your wife to be. (Take a moment and read the awesome testimony "Wife a New Woman" on our website or in our book *God Is Moving!* to see what true forgiveness will do to turn your marriage around and bring your wife home.) Stop looking at the bad things she is doing.

Replace that with asking God to show you how YOU have been the one at fault since you are or should be the head of your home, the spiritual leader, and therefore the one totally responsible for where your wife is and what she has done. (Once again take a moment and read the awesome testimony "Wife a New Woman" on our website or in our book *God Is Moving!* to see how taking the entire blame for your situation will free your wife to come back to you!!)

If your wife has left you, don't call her! **But** if *you* have left your wife or made her leave your home, *you* **must call her** and ask for her forgiveness. This point is critical! The longer you wait the greater the possibility of adultery, if it hasn't occurred already. (Please read the testimonies on our website which provide evidence of how these very principles worked in the lives of the men and women who followed them.)

Once you have repented to your wife, then DO NOT keep repenting and taking the ENTIRE blame for the situation. This can be counterproductive. Also, whether your wife accepts your apology or not is not the issue. You are doing it out of humility and obedience to God, nothing more.

Speak kindly and lovingly to your wife when you have an opportunity to talk with her. "Pleasant words are as honeycomb, sweet to the soul and healing to the bones." Prov. 16:24. "A joyful heart is good medicine, but a broken spirit dries up the bones." Prov. 17:22, Prov. 18:14. **You don't have to be joyful about your situation; just be joyful that God has it all under His control.** "All *discipline* for the moment seems not to be joyful, but sorrowful; yet to those who have been trained by it, afterwards it yields the peaceful fruit of righteousness." Hebr. 12:11.

Don't listen to any gossip or anyone who tries to give you bad reports about your wife. "Love bears all things, *believes all things*, hopes all things, endures all things. Love never fails." 1Cor. 13:7. Maybe your wife says she's not involved with anyone else, yet you KNOW she is. Nevertheless, you must believe her. Don't question or doubt her word. You're not being stupid or naive; you are expressing unconditional or agape love.

Sometimes it is your family or closest friends who try to persuade you to pursue divorce or tell your wife off for the things she has done or is doing. You must separate yourself from those who attempt to lead you astray from God by feeding your flesh and emotions. "Leave the presence of a fool or you will not discern words of knowledge." Prov. 14:7. "He who goes about as a slanderer reveals secrets; therefore do not associate with a gossip." Prov. 20:19. If you slander your wife, others will slander your wife too! "Whoever secretly slanders his neighbor, him I will destroy." Ps. 101:5.

Because you will receive much advice that is contrary to the will and the Word of God, don't share your situation with anyone! Ultimately it will arouse anger or self-pity in you! These emotions are of the flesh and will war against your spirit. God says in Gal. 5:17, "For the flesh sets its desire against the Spirit, and the Spirit against the flesh; for these are in opposition to one another, so that you may not do the things that you please."

Listening, discussing or seeking counsel for your situation will also bring in confusion since most Christians do NOT really KNOW the Word of God and even pastors may advise you contrary to God's Word! Unless they have "walked on the same water" they may disregard or minimize God's principles when you desperately need the entire **uncompromised** Word of God to save your marriage!

Do NOT try to find out what your wife is up to. If you do suspect there is someone else, or you KNOW that there is someone else she is involved with, then do what God says: "Let your eyes look directly in front of you. Watch the path of your feet, and all your ways will be established." Prov. 4:25. "Do not be afraid of sudden fear nor the onslaught of the wicked when it comes; for the Lord will be your confidence, and will keep your foot from being caught." Prov. 3:25-26. And again remember, love "BELIEVES all things." 1Cor. 13:7.

Do NOT confront your wife or the others involved! That is a net that Satan has left. So many men and women fall into this trap time and again. Watch out! You may satisfy your flesh but the consequences will destroy you and any feelings your wife may still have for you. Don't talk to the OM over the phone or in person.

So often men erroneously think that they should confront their wives because she shouldn't get away with it or should "know that I know." ALL who have confronted their wives or husbands, out of ignorance or by ignoring this book or this personal warning, have written to tell us how much they regret it! They ALL have shared that it resulted in MANY horrible consequences! Please don't be like Adam who went ahead and did what he knew he shouldn't!

Once the sin is out in the open it will be flaunted in front of your face, and you will lose the advantage that God has given you. You must remember, "Love **believes** all things." 1Cor. 13:7.

You must also remember at all times that this is a "spiritual" war. As in all wars, it is foolish and dangerous to let the enemy know what you know. No battle in the Bible was ever won by revealing inside information from the Lord! Nor does the Bible tell us to reveal enemy movements. Instead, it warns us to fight this as a spiritual war! 1Tim. 1:18 says to "fight the good fight." "We do not war according to the flesh." 2Cor. 10:3. We are told instead to "Be of sober spirit [which literally means WAKE UP], be on the alert. Your adversary, the devil, prowls about like a roaring lion, seeking someone to devour." 1Pet. 5:8.

Your wife, and others, are working with the devil, as slaves, to destroy your marriage, future and children. "Do you not know that when you present yourselves to someone as **slaves** for obedience, you are slaves of the one whom you obey, either of *sin resulting in death*, or of obedience resulting in righteousness?" Rom. 6:16. To win this war, YOU must be a slave of righteousness – therefore DO NOT confront her about her sin or what you know!!

Do NOT try to find out where your wife is if she hasn't given you her whereabouts! This is God's protection for you! Be quiet; be still.

Go into your prayer closet and begin to fight the battle through prayer, on your knees before the Lord. God can change your wife's heart, but you will harden it if you openly reveal mistrust, suspicion and jealousy. "The king's heart is like channels of water in the hand of the LORD; He turns it wherever He wishes." Prov. 21:1. The other man will then appear to be the one she wants, not you! Every wife will run to the defense of the man she is involved with when her husband verbally (or physically) attacks the OM. Take control of your emotions.

A wife will NOT respond to a man who is angry or one who is effeminate and cries. You must be humble, kind, and loving AND have complete control over your emotions. Afterwards, when you are alone, you can deal with your feelings. But in her presence, do not show unfavorable emotions.

Don't act hastily in ANY decision. At this time you are not thinking clearly and are most certainly acting on emotion rather than wisdom. "And he who makes haste with his feet errs." Prov. 19:2. "The prudent man considers his steps." Prov. 14:15. "There is a way which seems right to a man, but its end is the way of death." Prov. 16:25 and Prov. 14:12. "Do you see a man hasty in his words? There is more hope for a fool than for him." Prov. 29:20.

"The lot is cast into the lap, but its every decision is from the Lord." Prov. 16:33. "A wise man is cautious and turns away from evil." Prov. 14:16. Don't hurry to make changes like setting up a "visitation schedule." Don't be quick to run to get a divorce. God says, "I hate divorce." Mal. 2:16. Don't move out or leave your home: "Like a bird that wanders from her nest, so is a man who wanders from his home." Prov. 27:8.

Have you spoken to your wife about your needs, your concerns or your problems – only to have *her* reject you? Memorize these Scriptures: "My **God** shall supply all my needs according to His riches in glory." Phil. 4:19. "I would have despaired unless I had believed that I would see the goodness of the Lord in the land of the living. Wait on the Lord, be of good courage, yes, wait *on the Lord*." Ps. 27:13.

A man should be self-assured if he is to win his wife back to him. This is not pride, for it should be done with humility. If your wife has left then your home was out of order. Make sure you get the men's manual *A Wise Man* to learn how the home was designed to be.

"When a man's ways are pleasing to the Lord, He makes even his enemies to be at peace with him." Prov. 16:7. Instead of trying to convince your wife to return to you, take this opportunity to thank your wife and praise her for how she has cared for you, your children and your home in the past. This is God's way; it's called contentment.

Part of your problem may be your wife's career outside the home. Even though God says to wait, you may have moved ahead and bought things on credit or moved to a larger home and then believed your wife "needed to go to work." Then your house **sat empty** while your wife worked, and your children were in day care. Satan is a thief!

Soon you may lose the house that you worked so hard for. Allow God to save your home, your family and your marriage. (Please read Chapter 8, "Manages His Household" in *A Wise Man*.)

Did you ever encourage or tell your wife to leave? We at Restore Ministries have seen too many who have asked their spouses to leave or who have been first to mention the word "divorce" in a time of anger. When you plant bad seeds, don't be surprised if she ends up in adultery. Words have more power than you know. "And I say to you, that every careless word that men shall speak, they shall render account for it in the day of judgment." Matt. 12:36.

Maybe you wanted her to leave because of alcohol, drugs, arguments or unfaithfulness. Or maybe one of you just felt that you didn't love the other any more. Please read Chapter 15, "Comfort Those" for more help. Be aware that many men consider women who are out of their homes to be "single" even though they are **not**! Separation is the first step to divorce. And divorce is a life-changing mistake.

Many Christians, ignorant of the destruction of separation, advise those with marriage troubles to tell their wives who are unfaithful to leave or to not allow them to return home. Older men, as stated in Titus 2, should **"speak the things which are fitting for sound doctrine**...to be temperate, dignified, sensible, sound in faith, in love, in perseverance." Titus 2:1-2.

The separation that is spoken of in 1Cor. 7:5 is to be done with mutual agreement AND for the purpose of fasting and prayer. This verse confirms this: "if any brother has a wife who is an unbeliever [or a believer], and she consents to live with him, **let him not send her away."** 1Cor. 7:12.

By making a decision to separate or divorce, you will have chosen to destroy not only your life and your wife's life, but also your children's lives and future. Your (future) grandchildren, your parents and all your friends will also feel the devastating effects of this selfish, ignorant and foolish decision.

By suggesting that your wife leaves, you have taken that first step toward divorce. Isn't it time to turn around before things go any further? The world and Satan have convinced you that this separation or divorce will make things better, but that **is a lie!** If that were true, 8 out of 10 people wouldn't get divorced in that second or subsequent marriage. Once again, the Bible is clear: "any brother who has a wife who is an unbeliever [or a believer], and she consents to live with him, **let him not send her away."** 1Cor. 7:12.

However, if your wife has left you, you must stop pursuing, pressing her or even standing in her way. She will only try harder to get away from you or run to evil. "How blessed is the man who does not walk in the counsel of the wicked, nor stand in the WAY of sinners." Ps. 1:1. The only roadblock should be a "hedge of thorns." Hosea 2:6. You should read the book of Hosea in your Bible. We have written a prayer for you to memorize based on the hedge of thorns. (You will find it in Chapter 15, "I Searched for a Man.") Pray it daily *for* your wife.

Many ministries encourage "standers" to continue to pursue the spouse who has left with phone calls, cards, letters and statements about their "marriage covenant." THIS IS NOT SCRIPTURAL and has caused many to become "standers for life"! The Bible says, "if the unbelieving one leaves, **let him leave**; the brother or the sister is not under bondage in such cases, but God has **called us to peace**." 1Cor. 7:15. If you won't let go, friction will continue. "How blessed is the man who does not walk in the counsel of the wicked, nor **stand in the way of sinners**." Ps. 1:1, NIV. You must let your wife know that she is free to leave (based on 1Cor. 7:15). This will cause her to stop running, pursuing divorce or jumping into another marriage!

But I am already divorced. It's never too late even if a divorce has taken place. Many "remarry" their former spouses AFTER they have divorced. "Don't be overcome with evil, but overcome evil with good." Rom. 12:21. God specifically asked His prophet Hosea to remarry his wife Gomer even after she was blatantly unfaithful to him. "For she is not my wife, and I am not her husband." Hosea 2:2. "Then she will say, 'I will go back to my first husband, for it was better for me then than now.' " Hosea 2:7. "Then the Lord said to me (Hosea), 'Go again, love a woman who is loved by her husband, yet an adulteress.' " Hosea 3:1. God used the story of Hosea and Gomer to show His commitment to His own bride (the church) and His strong stand on marriage.

It also gives an example of how to allure your wife through the kind and loving way you speak to her. But, this is done AFTER she knows she is free to go. "Therefore, behold, I will allure her, bring her into the wilderness, and speak kindly to her." Hosea 2:14.

Don't allow your children to see your pain or anger toward your wife. Do ALL that you can to shield your children from what is going on. Otherwise they will develop bad feelings toward their mother.

Don't blame your wife for what has happened; instead, take the FULL responsibility and tell your children where the real fault lies. Be careful where you turn your children's hearts. Turning your children's hearts against your wife by what you say will destroy your children and break your wife's heart. Hurting the woman you love will never bring her home. Instead, love her by building her up in your children's eyes and cover her nakedness lest your children be cursed. "And Ham, the father of Canaan, saw the nakedness of his father, and **told** his two brothers outside… So he said, '**Cursed** be Canaan; a servant of servants he shall be to his brothers.' He also said, '**Blessed** be the LORD, the God of Shem; and let Canaan be his servant.'" Gen. 9:22, 25-26. Bless your children with kind, loving, forgiving and honoring words.

The Lord has allowed these trials in your life, and your children's lives, for a time, in order to draw you all closer to Him, accomplish His work in all of you and then draw you back together again for His glory! When your wife is not around to blame, you can then look at yourself and look to Him to change you! When you seek Him, you will become closer to Him; then He will change you more into His image! "They looked to Him and were radiant, and their faces shall never be ashamed." Ps. 34:5.

Don't allow your children to speak badly about their mother. You must demand respect for their mother (whether they are 5, 15 or 25!). "Honor your father and your **mother**." Exod. 20:12, Deut. 5:16, Mark 7:10. If you have spoken badly about their mother, first ask God for forgiveness, next humbly ask your wife's forgiveness and lastly ask your children's forgiveness. "He who conceals his transgression will not prosper." Prov. 28:13. Then begin to build her up in the children's (and your) eyes. (See Chapter 4, "Thrusts of a Sword" for more knowledge.)

Remember, you will have trouble with your children honoring you if you dishonor *your* wife! 1Pet. 3:7 tells us, "You husbands likewise, live with your wives in an understanding way, as with a weaker vessel, since she is a woman; and **grant her honor** as a fellow heir of the grace of life, so that *your prayers may not be hindered.*"

Don't allow your children to become unruly. "A foolish son is a grief to his father, and bitterness to her who bore him." Prov. 17:25.

"A child who gets his own way brings shame to his mother." Prov. 29:15. Don't cause yourself grief or cause your wife to become bitter or shame her. Instead of allowing your children to vent their anger, use this time to teach them to forgive and pray for their mother.

When the anger is gone, the pain will be felt; then teach them to rely on God for comfort. This Scripture helped my (then) 5-year-old when he memorized it: "For He has said 'I will never leave you nor forsake you.' " Hebr. 13:5. Your children are confused right now, so give them clear directions. (See Lesson 14, "Your Father's Instructions" in *A Wise Man* for more knowledge.) Again, you will have trouble enforcing this if *you* exhibit a lack of control of your anger.

Be careful not to choose the "easiest" road. It may *seem* like the easiest road, but in the end it is the road to even more sadness, trials, difficulties and heartache than you are now experiencing. We, who have gone through difficult marriages, separation and/or divorce, want to warn you against any ideas, books or other people who will sway you to go the way of the world, which *ALWAYS* ends in disaster! If the world endorses it, as Christians we know it is the wide road to destruction.

Narrow is the way that leads to life, and few are those who find it! "Enter by the narrow gate; for the gate is wide, and the way is broad that leads to destruction, and many are those who enter by it. For the gate is small, and the way is narrow that leads to life, and few are those who find it." Matt. 7:13-14. You must look for that narrow way in all your decisions, in the way you speak to others, and in the way you handle the trials that WILL come your way now and in the future.

Please be careful what you read. The books whose foundation is in philosophy or those written by psychologists or marriage counselors can fill your mind with destructive thoughts. Be careful about reading books that cover such topics as "tough love," "spicing up your marriage," and "co-dependency." We have seen the damage that these ideas have done to marriages and the men and women who have looked to them in their desperation. Instead, renew your mind with God's Word. If you meditate on His Word, God promises in Psalm 1 that you will prosper in everything that you do!!

Look to God and to those of "like mind" to encourage you to believe God for your marriage. Please go to the Counselor (God's Word), which is free, and save your money and your marriage. God wants you to Himself! Stay away from the "professionals." Every professional has his/her ways and beliefs. There are thousands of both Christian and secular marriage counselors and books about marriage solutions. If they knew all the answers, why is there an epidemic of divorce, especially in the church?!!

Where do you begin? What should you do? Begin to move your demolished house onto the rock. "Therefore everyone who hears these words of Mine, and acts upon them, may be compared to a wise man, who built his house upon the rock. And the rain descended, and the floods came, and the winds blew, and burst against that house; and yet it did not fall, for it had been founded upon the rock." Matt. 7:25. "By wisdom a house is built, and by understanding it is established; and by knowledge the rooms are filled with all precious and pleasant riches." Prov. 24:3.

Praise God in *ALL* things. "Let us continually offer up a **sacrifice** of praise to God, that is, the fruit of lips that give thanks to His name." Hebr. 13:15. "Rejoice in the Lord **always**; again I will say, rejoice!" Phil. 4:4.

Learn to really pray. "And I searched for a man among them who should build up the wall and **stand in the gap** before Me for the land, that I should not destroy it; but I found no one." Ezek. 22:30. Standing in the gap does NOT mean standing in your wife's way! It means praying for her as you would pray for yourself.

Take every thought captive. "We are destroying speculations and every lofty thing raised up against the knowledge of God, and we are taking every thought captive to the obedience of Christ." 2Cor. 10:5.

Begin to renew your mind to be like Christ's and to look down at your situation as God does, from above. Get *A Wise Man Builds* and work through it with a friend. Get a "Bible Promise Book" from your local Christian bookstore (very inexpensive) and put it next to your bed. The verses will become a place of refuge for you as you pore over His promises when you become anxious.

Get 3x5 cards and write down Bible verses that you can use to renew your mind, to fight in the Spirit (the sword of the Spirit is the Word of God), or to run to when you experience an attack of fear, doubt or lies. Keep these with you and read them over and over again. Stop thinking and talking so much about your problems; listen to God and read His Word.

As we said, Psalm 1 gives you a promise: "His delight is in the law of the Lord, and in His law he meditates day and night. And he will be like a tree firmly planted by streams of water, which yields its fruit in its season, and its leaf does not wither; and in whatever he does, he prospers." Practically speaking, if you read and reread this book to the point of wearing it out or take the time to make 3x5 cards with the Scriptures you need, you can't help but meditate on His Word. Almost every man I have known who has a restored marriage did one or both of these things.

NO marriage is too far gone! "With men this is impossible, but with God all things are possible." Matt. 19:26. Again remember that it is not true that you *and* your wife, together, must seek help to change the marriage. We have seen the good "fruits" of the men who have asked God to change their wives' hearts, to work on them, and God was faithful. (See "fruits," Matt. 7:16, 20.)

"And why do you look at the speck that is in your brother's eye, but do not notice the log that is in your own eye? Or how can you say to your brother, 'Let me take the speck out of your eye,' and behold, the log is in your own eye? You hypocrite, first take the log out of your own eye, and then you will see clearly to take the speck out of your brother's eye." Matt. 7:3, Luke 6:41. We pray the same for you: that you will see clearly how to really help your wife by being a godly man who is meek, yet bold in the spirit, who allures his wife with kind and loving words.

How long? Many men have asked us "how long" their wife will be gone or "how long" their trial will continue. It may help you if you think about it as a journey. How long it takes often depends on you. As the Lord shows you an area that He is working on, work "with Him." Do not become sidetracked by work or everyday life. Satan will bring in "the cares of the world" in order to choke the Word out of you. He also will bring situations, emergencies and other crises that will divert your attention away from your destination –- your restored family!

Too often our journey seems to have "stalled." Just take the next step of obedience. When you become weary with the "wait," do not lose heart. This is the time our Lord is using to stretch our faith and focus our attention on His working in our lives. All that is required is our obedience, which will release spiritual power to work on our behalf. It is not necessary that God give us a detailed explanation of what He is doing. We know that He will work out His purposes through whatever happens even when we have made a mistake. We must believe that He is working with people and situations and arranging circumstances for His good for us.

There Is MORE Help!

Another book that you will find helpful in your desire to restore your marriage is our men's manual *A Wise Man*. This book is available on our website to read or print off for FREE, or if you prefer, it can be ordered in book form on our website: **www.RestoreMinistries.net**.

Though we no longer minister to men, with the exception of our two books for men, let us still pray for you now...

"Dear Lord, please guide this special brother during the trouble in his marriage. And his ears shall hear a word behind him saying, this is the way, walk here, when he turns to his right and when he turns to his left. (Isa. 30:21)

"Please reassure him when he sees a thousand fall on his right side and ten thousand at his left; help him to know that if he follows You, it will not happen to him. (Ps. 91:7) Hide him under your protective wings.

"Help him to find the narrow path that will lead him to life, the abundant life you have for him, for his wife and for his family. Lord, I pray for a testimony when this troubled or broken marriage is healed and restored that You can use for Your glory! We will give You all the honor and the glory. Amen."

We are the Clay

"We are the Clay,
and Thou our potter;
And all of us are the work of Thy hand."
Isaiah 64:8

When you are going through a marriage crisis it is so easy to focus on what your wife is doing to you. However, as long as you do this you will struggle and never come to victory. You will learn in an upcoming chapter, "Weapons of our Warfare," that your wife is not the enemy.

Let us learn, in this chapter, that God many times is not changing our wives because God is using the things our wives are doing as the potter's wheel and His hands to mold us more into His image. However, if we complain because we would rather He use something or someone else, not our wives, not finances, and not our marriages as His wheel, we will wander in the desert land for years!

Quarrel with his Maker? " 'Woe to the one who **quarrels with his Maker**' – An earthenware vessel among the vessels of earth! Will the clay say to the potter, 'What are you doing?' Or the thing you are making say, 'He has no hands'?" Isa. 45:9. Let God be God. Instead of complaining about "how" or "whom" He uses to irritate us into finally seeking Him to change us – praise Him for His faithfulness! He is determined to bring you forth as a handsome vessel ready for **His** use.

But you don't understand. Many men tell us, as we try to encourage them, that we "just don't understand!" In many ways we *do* understand, yet they are right that no one except Jesus really understands. "Shall the potter be considered as equal with the clay, that what is made should say to its maker, **'He has no**

understanding'?" Isa. 29:16. Talk to Him about your situation and allow Him to give you peace. He knows what's best for you, so work with Him.

You are in His hand. "Behold, like the clay in the potter's hand, so are you **in My hand**." Jer. 18:6. Isn't it comforting to know that you are in God's Hand? Though your wife may tell you that she doesn't care for you anymore, or treat you as if she doesn't, your Lord does. Who else do you need? The truth is that your wife does care. She is hurt and deceived, but she does care for you down beneath those hurts.

God's Prescription

God has a prescription for healing a nation or a family. He says "If My people who are called by My name **humble** themselves and **pray**, and **seek My face** and **turn from their wicked ways**, then I will *hear* from heaven, will *forgive* their sin, and will *heal* their land." 2Chr. 7:14.

God told us that if we **humble** ourselves, pray, seek His face (not His hand) AND turn from our wicked ways, THEN HE WILL hear, forgive and heal us. Instead, we "walk in the counsel of the wicked" (Ps. 1:1) and "trust in mankind" (Jer. 17:5), so now we suffer the consequences – superficial healing! "The brokenness of His people is healed superficially." Jer. 8:11. "And they have healed the brokenness of My people superficially, saying, 'Peace, peace,' but there is no peace." Jer. 6:14.

Instead we are to die to self. "...and He died for all that they who live should no longer live **for themselves**, but *for Him* who died and rose again on *their behalf.*" 2Cor. 5:15.

Only the Humble

Humble yourself. Self-willed, haughty people understand the Word without the Spirit, but to know the mind of God we need **humility**!

Humility will be tested. "...He might **humble** you, **testing** you, to know *what was in your heart*, whether you would *keep His commandments* or not." Deut. 8:2.

Humility will save you. "When you are **cast down**, you will *speak with confidence* and the **humble** person He will **save**." Job 22:29.

Humility will strengthen your heart. "O Lord, Thou hast **heard** the *desire* of the **humble**; Thou wilt
strengthen their heart, Thou wilt *incline Thine ear*." Ps. 10:17.

Only the humble will be exalted. "He has brought down rulers from their thrones, and has **exalted** those who were **humble**." Luke 1:52.

Only the humble will be given the grace that they need. "But He gives a greater grace. Therefore it says, 'GOD IS OPPOSED TO THE PROUD, BUT **GIVES GRACE** TO THE **HUMBLE**.' Humble yourselves in
the presence of the Lord, and He will exalt you." Jas. 4:6, 10.

Humility is rooted in the spirit. "To sum up, let all be harmonious, sympathetic, brotherly, kindhearted, and **humble *in spirit***." 1Pet. 3:8. Your false humility will be manifested in a self-righteous attitude. It will surface in anger and bitterness toward your wife and others.

Spiritual arrogance. Over half of those who come to our ministry for help to restore their marriages exhibit spiritual arrogance or self-righteousness. This is what we refer to as a Pharisee spirit. Men, this is so dangerous. It WILL prevent God from moving your marriage toward restoration and it is what is really driving your wife away.

God showed us, in His Word, that Jesus was only harsh, critical, and opposed to one set of individuals – the Pharisees! There are so many Christians who pretend to be spiritual on the outside but are filthy on the inside. There are so many Christians who look at their wives' sins yet neglect to look at the logs in their own eyes. Is this you? Do you look at what your wife has done or is doing and neglect to see your anger, bitterness, harshness and arrogance?

Others may look at you now as the "poor victim" who has been walked out on and cheated on. Do they see you as the one desperately trying to hold your marriage together? Are you seen as the one waiting, with open arms, to forgive your wife, "the sinner," "the harlot," when she comes to her senses by repenting and coming back home from the far country! Scribe, Pharisee, "white-washed tomb"!!

If you can identify with this sinful and prideful mindset, if this is you, I would beg you to get on your face before God and ask Him to cleanse you of this attitude that will not only inhibit restoration, but will also put you in opposition to a sincere and intimate relationship with God.

Pray! Begin by praying Psalm 51:2-4. "Wash me thoroughly from my iniquity, and cleanse me from my sin. For I know my transgressions, and my sin is ever before me. Against Thee, Thee only, I have sinned, and done what is evil in Thy sight, so that Thou art justified when Thou dost speak, and blameless when Thou dost judge." There is much more on praying in the last two chapters of this book.

Seek My face. "If My people who are called by My name humble themselves and pray, and **seek My face**..." 2Chr. 7:13. "Seek the Lord and His strength; **Seek His face** *continually*." 1Chr. 16:11. "...**seek My face**; in their affliction they will **earnestly** seek Me." Hosea 5:15.

They were radiant. "They **looked to Him** and were **radiant**, and their faces shall never be ashamed." Ps. 34:5. Seek His face! So many seek His hand (what He can do for "me"). But those who seek the face of God will inherit all things!

Turn from your wicked ways. "If My people who are called by My name humble themselves and pray, and seek My face and **turn from their wicked ways**..." 2Chr. 7:13. Scriptures are not only for the head; they are for the heart and the will. To get the real impact of Scripture, we must surrender our lives and our wills to the leading of the Spirit. We must be willing to be made over. We must yield to Him.

To obey is better than sacrifice. "Behold, to **obey is better than sacrifice**, and to heed than the fat of rams. For rebellion is as the sin of divination, and insubordination is as iniquity and idolatry." 1Sam. 15:22. Do you know the right thing to do, yet you do not do it? Obey Him! "Therefore, to one who knows the right thing to do, and does not do it, to him it is sin." Jas. 4:17.

Walk in the Spirit

Walk in the Spirit. Being filled with the Holy Spirit will enable you to walk in the Spirit, not in sin or fleshly desires. Ask God to FILL you with His Holy Spirit right now! "And I will put **My Spirit** within you and *cause* you to *walk* in **My statutes**, and you will be careful to **observe My ordinances**." Ezek. 36:27. "But I say, **walk by the Spirit**, and you will not carry out the **desire of the flesh**." Gal. 5:16.

Pray. "If My people who are called by My name humble themselves and **pray**…" 2Chr. 7:13-16.

We can always trust God to bring about everything for our good if "…we know that God causes all things to work together for good to those who **love God**, to those who are called according to **His purpose**." Rom. 8:28.

What "Condition" Needs to Be Met to Be Heard?

Conform your desires to His will. Jesus' promise is based on this condition: "If you abide in Me, and My words abide in you, ask whatever you wish, and it shall be done for you." John 15:7. When your heart rests in Jesus alone and *your will* is centered in *His will*, you are truly making Him Lord. And to know His will is to know His Word. It is His will that your marriage be healed. He hates divorce and we are to be reconciled; however, He has conditions.

The condition for every blessing. Each promise given by God has a condition for that blessing. Many will claim a portion of the Scripture, yet omit or overlook the conditions.

Condition: "Believe on the Lord Jesus...
Promise: and you shall be saved." Acts 16:31.

Condition: "Delight yourself in the Lord...
Promise: and He will give you the desires of your heart." Ps. 37:4.

Condition: "Train up a child in the way he should go...
Promise: Even when he is old he will not depart from it." Prov. 22:6.

Condition: First, "to those who love God." And secondly, "to those who are called according to His purpose."
Promise: "And we know that God causes all things to work together for good...." Rom. 8:28.

Personal commitment: to allow God to change me. "Based on what I have learned from God's Word, I commit to allowing God to change me through whatever means or through whomever He chooses. I will focus my attention on changing myself rather than my wife or others around me."

Date: _____ Signed: _____

Chapter 3

Have Faith in God

And Jesus answered them,
"Have faith in God."
Mark 11:22

Do You Have Faith or Fear?

Fear will be one of the greatest attacks that you will need to overcome. Rom. 12:21 tells us, "Do not be overcome by evil, but overcome evil with good." Fear will steal your faith and make you totally vulnerable to the enemy. When you listen to all that others tell you about what your wife is doing, not doing, or is planning to do, instead of keeping your eyes on the Lord and His Word, you will fail to focus on Him and you will begin to sink!

And you must speak the "truth" to everyone always about your faith in God's ability and His desire to restore your marriage. Again, read the testimonies of restored marriages; then BELIEVE that yours will be added to theirs!

An example of faith, Peter. Read the account of Peter in Matthew 14 starting in verse 22. Jesus asked Peter to walk on water. If He is asking you to walk on water, are you going to get out of the boat? Watch when Peter cries out to Jesus – it is always followed by the word **immediately**. Immediately, Jesus spoke to them and told them to take courage. Then later when Peter began to sink and he cried out to the Lord, "immediately Jesus stretched out His hand and took hold of him!" Matt. 14:31.

Fear. A question we must ask ourselves is "why did Peter sink?" "But seeing the wind, he became afraid." Matt. 14:30. If you look at your situation and at the battle that is raging before you, you will sink! Peter took his eyes off the Lord and the result was fear! It says, "he became afraid." If you take your eyes off the Lord, you will become fearful.

Your testimony. Another very important point is to see what happened to the others who were in the boat. (Did you forget that there were others who didn't get out of the boat?) It says, "And those who were in the boat worshiped Him saying, 'You are certainly God's Son!' " Matt. 14:33. Are you willing to allow God to use you to show His goodness, His loving kindness, His protection, and to draw others to Him? There is a great reward! This is evangelism. Others will come to you when they are having trouble because they have seen your peace despite your circumstances.

Overcome

The wind stopped. "And when they got into the boat, the wind stopped." Matt. 14:32. Your battle will not go on forever. This test was needed to make Peter strong enough to be the "Rock" of which Jesus had spoken. (Matt. 16:18) Satan (and others working for him) will tell you that you will stay in the trial unless you get away, or give in and give up.

God never intended us to remain "In the valley of the shadow of death." In Proverbs 23 it says that we go "*through* the valley of the shadow of death." Satan wants us to think that God wants us **to live there**! He wants to paint a "hopeless" picture! God is our hope, and hope is the faith in His Word that has been sown in our hearts.

Faith

Abraham. A second example is when Abraham was 90 years old and still without the child God had promised him. It says, "He hoped against hope." (Rom. 4:18) Isn't that awesome? Even when all hope was gone, he continued to believe God and take Him at His Word. We *must* do the same.

Act on the faith that you have. "And He said to them, 'Because of the littleness of your faith; for truly I say to you, if you have **faith as a mustard seed**, you shall say to this mountain, 'Move from here to there,' and it shall move; and *nothing* shall be impossible to you.' " Matt. 17:20.

If you lack faith. If you lack faith, you should ask God for it. There is a battle, even for our faith. "Fight the good **fight of faith**...." 1Tim. 6:12. And "I have fought the **good fight**, I have finished the course, I have kept the **faith**...." 2Tim. 4:7 "And He (Jesus) could do **no miracle** there except that He laid His hands upon a few sick people and healed them. And He wondered at their **unbelief**." Mark 6:5. When the Lord lays His hands on you and your marriage, will He marvel at YOUR unbelief?

Imitators of faith. We would do well to imitate those in Scripture who exhibited faith (you can find the Hall of Faith in Hebrews chapter 11). We need to act on God's promises. "...but **imitators** of those who through **faith and patience** *inherit the promises*." Heb. 6:12. There are many men who have followed the principles found in this book who have had victory over troubled or even broken marriages. Their testimonies will encourage you in your faith. Believe as the song says, "What He's done for others, He'll do for you!" Read all the incredible testimonies of marriages that God restored on our website at: www.MarriageHelpOnline.com.

Doubt Destroys

Double-minded or doubting. You must not be double-minded. Your mind must not waver or doubt God. "But let him **ask in faith** *without any doubting,* for the one who doubts is like the surf of the sea driven and tossed by the wind. For let not that man expect that he will receive anything from the Lord, being a double- minded man, *unstable in all his ways*." Jas. 1:6-8. "I **hate** those who are **double-minded**, But I love Thy law." Ps. 119:13.

If you have trouble with double-mindedness, you need to read and meditate on God's Word, which is the only truth! You MUST also separate yourself from ANYONE who continues to tell you something contrary to your desire or God's ability to restore your marriage. You will learn in the upcoming chapter "Desires of Your Heart" that it doesn't matter about your wife's will to leave you and be with someone else. What matters is her heart. So be bold and speak the "truth" to everyone always about your faith in God's ability and His desire to restore your marriage.

Faith without works. "But someone may well say, 'You have faith, and I have works; show me your faith without the works, and I will **show you my faith** *by* **my works.**' " Jas. 2:18. Show others that you have faith by your actions. If you believe that your wife will return to you, act like it. Make SURE you wear your wedding ring. Stop walking around like there is no hope. Don't make plans that are not based on your marriage being restored! "But are you willing to recognize, you *foolish fellow*, that **faith without works is useless**?" Jas. 2:20.

Firm in your faith. Remind yourself of those who overcame and thus received the abundant life God promised. "But resist him, **firm in your faith**, knowing that the **same experiences** of suffering are being accomplished by your brethren who are in the world." 1Pet. 5:9. Read and reread the testimonies on our website and in our book "*God is Moving!*" Keep the testimonies of others in the forefront of your mind. Those who believed God and never gave up now have a restored marriage. Share these testimonies with your family and friends who doubt that your marriage can be saved or that God can break the relationship she is in and turn her heart back to you.

How to Increase Your Faith

Faith. Read about different difficult situations in the Bible and identify your situation with theirs. Read how Jesus stilled the waves of the sea, to learn of His great power. (Mark 4:39) Read then how He fed the five thousand with the five barley loaves and two small fish, to know that He can do so much with very little. (John 6:1-15) Read how Jesus cleansed the lepers (Luke 17:11-17), healed the sick, opened the eyes of the blind (John 9:1-41), and forgave the fallen woman (John 8:3-11), so you will never doubt His mercy for you and your situation. Again, read the testimonies of restored marriages; then BELIEVE yours will be added to theirs!

The Word. How can we gain faith, or increase our faith? "So **faith comes from hearing, and hearing by the *Word* of Christ.**" Rom. 10:17. Read His Word and the testimonies of others. Surround yourself with faithful *men* who will believe with you. Those who have stood for God will teach you and hold you up. Many times we find that when you feel like you are almost out of faith, you should give away what little you have left. When God brings you in contact with another man who is having marriage trouble, encourage him and give him the rest of your faith. You will walk away rejoicing because God will fill you **full** of faith. (Please be very careful to only encourage and share your faith with other men - not women. We have seen more than one man fall into adultery this way.) Read 1Kgs. 17:12-15 to remember the widow who gave her last cake to Elijah and the miracle *she* received!

So many come to us for help and fail to reap a restored marriage because they feel they are unable to sow into anyone else's life as they are struggling to save their own marriage. This is unbiblical and contrary to God's principles. Get yourself an Encouragement Partner by joining our Restoration Fellowship and help him restore his marriage. All you need is one other man who is trying to restore his marriage. God will use you powerfully as you minister to other men in your pain and lack – and God will bless your efforts with "a peace that surpasses all understanding" and a restored marriage!

Obedience. Don't forget that obedience to God is paramount to victory. Don't forget what Jesus said, "Not everyone who says to Me, 'Lord, Lord,' will enter the kingdom of heaven; but he who does the will of My Father who is in heaven. And then I will declare to them, 'I never knew you; DEPART FROM ME, YOU WHO PRACTICE LAWLESSNESS.' " Matt. 7:21, 23. If you "practice" or keep doing what you now know is contrary to the

Biblical principles found in this book – your marriage will NOT be restored!

In God's will. If your heart convicts you that you are not in God's will and that you are not following His principles, then of course you will have no confidence and no faith to receive your request from the Lord. Ask God to "break" you so your will will become His will.

You MUST Wait

Wait. Assuredly, there will be many "battles" that must be fought (and won) in the war against your marriage. Just remember, "When the battle is the Lord's, the victory is ours!"

Just like with all real wars, not all the battles are won by the same side so do not be discouraged if you have fallen short and made mistakes. We have the comfort of knowing that He hears us immediately, but His response may sometimes seem slow.

In the book of Daniel, an angel spoke to him and gave us these insights: "…from the **first day** that you **set your heart** on understanding this and on **humbling yourself** before God, *your words were heard,* and I have come in response to your words. But the prince of Persia was withstanding me for **twenty-one days**." Dan. 10:12-13. It may take some time to win the battles, so do not become weary. "But as for you, brethren, do not grow weary of **doing good**." 2Ths. 3:13.

His timing. One thing you must also understand is that God seems to work on ONE thing at a time. We must work *with* Him in His timing. This does not mean we need to **wait to pray;** it only means we need to wait for God to change the situation at the proper time. Thank God that He doesn't dump (through conviction) all our sins on top of us all at once! Just use the time while you wait to pray.

Personal commitment: to allow God to change me. "Based on what I have learned from God's Word, I commit to seeking God and His Word to increase my faith is His ability to restore my marriage. I will fight fear by keeping my eyes on Jesus the Author and Finisher of my faith."

Date: _____ Signed:_____

———— Chapter 4————

The Testing of Your Faith

"Consider it all joy, my brethren,
when you encounter various trials,
knowing that the testing of your faith
produces endurance."
James 1:2-3

What is **God's** purpose for our tests, temptations, trials and tribulations? Many Christians have no idea why God allows our sufferings. Without this understanding, is it any wonder why Christians today are so easily defeated? We will see that there are many **benefits** that come from our trials and tests, especially the building of our faith and the endurance needed to finish the course set before us.

The most important thing we need to realize during our tests, temptations, trials, and tribulations is that God **is** in control! It is **His** hand that allows these trials to touch us or not to touch us. When He does allow it, He sends His grace that enables us to endure it.

Permission for adversity. The most comforting thing to know is that Satan cannot touch us without God's permission. "Then the Lord said to Satan, 'Behold, all that he has is in your power, only **do not put forth your hand on him.**'" Job. 1:12. Satan not only needs permission, but he is also given specific instructions on how he can touch us. "Simon, Simon, behold, Satan has demanded permission to sift you like wheat...." Luke 22:31.

Temptations. The temptations that we experience, Scripture tells us, are common to man, yet God does provide a way of escape.

"No temptation has overtaken you but that which is **common to man**; and God is faithful, who will not allow you to be tempted beyond what you are able, but with the **temptation** will provide **the way of escape** also, *that you may be able to endure it.*" 1Cor. 10:13. He is not going to take you out of the fire until you are willing to walk in it, through it, and endure it!

Temptations are brought on by our own lusts. Lust is simply what WE want. Also God cannot tempt us to do evil, but instead it is our lusts that tempt us to do what we know we shouldn't! "Let no one say when he is being tempted, 'I am being **tempted by God**'; for God cannot be tempted by evil, and He Himself does not tempt anyone. But each one is tempted when he is carried away and **enticed by his own lust**." Jas. 1:13.

Repentance and salvation. "I now rejoice, not that you were made sorrowful, but that you were made sorrowful to the point of repentance; for you were made sorrowful according to the **will of God**, in order that you might not suffer loss in anything through us. For the sorrow that is according to the **will of God** produces a **repentance without regret**, leading to salvation; but the sorrow of the world produces death." 2Cor. 7:9. God allows us to be sorrowful to bring us to repentance. If you try to make your wife sorry for what she has done, it will not bring true and genuine repentance, but instead will HARDEN her heart toward God and you!

We need grace. "And He has said to me, 'My **grace** is sufficient for you, for power is perfected in weakness'. Most gladly, therefore, I will rather boast about my weaknesses, that the power of Christ may dwell in me. Therefore, I am **well content** with **weaknesses**, with **insults**, with **distresses**, with **persecutions**, with **difficulties**, for Christ's sake; for when I am weak, then I am strong." 2Cor. 12: 9-10. You will NEVER see restoration until you exhibit contentment in your trials.

Amazing Grace

How do we get the grace we need to make it through our trials? Through humility.

"God hates the proud but **gives grace** to the **humble**." Jas. 4:6.

"For everyone who exalts himself shall be **humbled**, but he who **humbles** himself shall be exalted." Luke 18:14.

"Blessed are the **humble** for they shall inherit the earth." Matt. 5:5.

"A man's pride will bring him low, but a **humble spirit** will obtain honor." Prov. 29:23.

Boasting about our weaknesses, confessing our faults and being humble will enable the Holy Spirit to dwell in us. Then we will learn contentment no matter what our circumstances. Once you are content in your situation, God can give you what you've been seeking – your wife back!

Learning contentment. We see that we must *learn* contentment by the difficult circumstances that God has allowed. "Not that I speak from want, for I have **learned** to be **content** in whatever circumstances I am. In every circumstance I have **learned the secret** of being filled and going hungry, both of having abundance and suffering need." Phil 4:11.

Learning obedience. Even Jesus learned obedience from His suffering. "Although He was a Son, He *learned* obedience from *the things* which He **suffered**." Heb. 5:8.

He will perfect us. "For I am confident of this very thing, that He who **began a good work in you** will **perfect** it until the day of Christ Jesus." Phil 1:6. Once He has begun a good work in you or your wife, **He** will complete it. And please don't try to play "Mr. holy spirit" with your wife! Do not be deceived; judging your wife or condemning her actions will never bring her to repentance – never!

We are to be a comfort to others. We are not merely to accept God's comfort – we are commanded to give that comfort to others, no matter what their affliction! "The God of all comfort, who comforts us in all our affliction so that we may be able to **comfort** those who are in **any affliction** with the comfort with which we ourselves are comforted by God." 2Cor. 1:3-4. Restore Ministries offers many opportunities for you to minister to those seeking restoration or you can begin to minister to others in your church.

Our Father's discipline. Many times our suffering is discipline for disobeying God's Law. "My son, do not regard lightly the **discipline** of the Lord, nor faint when you are being reproved by Him; for those whom the Lord loves He **disciplines** and He scourges *every* **son** whom He receives. It is for **discipline** that you **endure**; God deals with you as with sons. He **disciplines** us for our good, that we may **share His holiness.**" Heb. 12:5-10. When a trial comes into your day, ask yourself "Is this God disciplining me, or is He testing me to see how I am going to react?"

Discipline is a blessing. We must follow the examples of the prophets of the Bible to help others to endure their adversity. "As an example, brethren, of suffering and patience, take the prophets who spoke in the name of the Lord. Behold, we count those **blessed** who **endured.** You have heard of the **endurance** of Job and have seen the outcome of the Lord's dealings, that the Lord is full of compassion and is merciful." Jas. 5:10.

To receive a blessing. "But even if you should suffer for the sake of righteousness, you are **blessed.** And do not fear their intimidations and do not be troubled." 1Pet. 3:14. When evil is done to us or insults are cast our way, we must endure them, without returning them, or we will not receive our blessing. We need to remember that insults and evils are brought into our lives to give us an "opportunity" to receive a blessing.

1Pet. 3:9 says "Not returning evil for evil, or insult for insult, but **giving a blessing** instead, for you were called for the very purpose that you may inherit a **blessing.**" If you continue to respond with an insult or another evil, don't expect to be blessed. This is the first step. Secondly, you must ask the Lord to show you how you can bless the person who insulted you or did evil against you, only then will you inherit the blessing of a restored marriage.

Discipline may be sorrowful. Discipline is never joyful when you are in the midst of it. Yet, those who have been trained by His discipline know the rewards of righteousness – peace and a restored marriage. "All **discipline** for the moment seems not to be joyful, but sorrowful; yet to those who have been **trained** by it, afterwards it yields the peaceful fruit of righteousness." Heb. 12:11.

It begins with Christians. Why must suffering first begin with Christians? Because sinful, disobedient Christians will never draw others to the Lord. Again, it is the "will of God" that we are put though sufferings. We need to *allow* ourselves to suffer (usually at the hands of another, even our own spouse) by entrusting ourselves to God. "For it is time for judgment to **begin** with the household of God; and if it **begins** with us first, what will be the outcome for those who do not obey the gospel of God? Therefore, let those also who **suffer** according to the **will of God** entrust their souls to a faithful Creator in doing what is right." 1Pet. 4:17.

The power of our faith. It is our faith that opens the door to miracles. You need to believe that He is able to restore your marriage, and not doubt, in your heart. "And Jesus answered saying to them, 'Have **faith** in God. Truly I say to you, whoever says to this mountain, be taken up and cast into the sea, and **does not doubt it in his heart**, but **believes** that what he says is going to happen, it shall be granted him. Therefore I say to you, all things for which you pray, they shall be granted unto you.' " Mark 11:22-24.

God in His Word has told us that we *will* suffer. "For indeed when we were with you, we kept *telling you in advance* that we were going to *suffer affliction*; and so it came to pass, as you know. For this reason, when I could endure it no longer; I also sent to find out about your *faith*, for fear that the tempter might have tempted you, and our labor should be in vain." 1Thes. 3:4-5. What has happened in your marriage is NOT a sign that it is over. It is what

God used to get your attention and is now using to change you. Don't give up! Don't let Satan steal the miracle that God has for you when you have endured and prevailed!

With God. "With men this is impossible, but with God **all things are possible.**" Matt. 19:26. "Looking upon them, Jesus said, 'With men it is impossible, but not with God; for **all things are possible with God.**'" Mark 10:27. Nothing (NOT A THING) is impossible with God. Work *with* God. Don't make the mistake of having *your* plan and expecting God to bless it. You must work "with God." Be assured, He has the perfect plan.

What you speak. "...let us **hold fast our confession**." Heb. 4:14. "But sanctify Christ as Lord in your hearts, **always being ready** to make a defense to everyone *who asks you* to give an account of the **hope that is in you,** yet with gentleness and reverence." 1Pet. 3:15. "If it be so our God whom we serve is **able to deliver** us from the furnace of blazing fire; and He will deliver us out of your hand, O king. But **even if He does not**...." Dan. 3:17.

We need to speak what God says in His Word, without wavering, with hope on our lips. But wait until you are asked to give an account. You **will** be asked if you are filled with the joy of the Lord in the midst of your adversity! When asked about your hope regarding your marriage, be sure that you answer the other person with reverence, respect and gentleness. Never use Scripture to argue with anyone!

Gird your mind and stay fixed. "Therefore, **gird your minds** for action, keep **sober** in spirit, **fix your hope** completely on the **grace** to be brought to you at the revelation of Jesus Christ." 1Pet. 1:13. The word sober means to be clear thinking; be clear in your mind about what you really believe to avoid the consequences of double-mindedness.

Be joyful. We are to be joyful in our trials because we know they are producing endurance that will enable us to finish the course set before us. "Consider it all joy, my brethren, when you encounter **various trials**, knowing that the **testing of your faith** produces **endurance**. And let **endurance** have its perfect result, that you may be perfect and complete, lacking nothing. But if any of you lacks wisdom, let him ask of God, who gives it to all men without reproach, and it will be given to him. But let him ask **in faith without any doubting,** for the one who doubts is like the surf of the sea driven and tossed by the wind." Jas. 1:2-6.

Be prepared – your faith WILL be tested! Fears and doubts come into everyone's mind; just don't entertain them! Instead, think only good things. If you doubt, you will have trouble believing and the trials will become harder. And remember, we will have a "variety" of trials, some major and others mere irritations. We need to thank Him for **all** of our trials. This is our sacrifice of praise.

Rejoice. "Rejoice in the Lord always; again I say **rejoice! Let your forbearing spirit be known to all men**, the Lord is near! Be anxious for nothing, but in everything by prayer and supplication with **thanksgiving** let your requests be made known to God. And the peace of God, which surpasses all comprehension, shall guard your hearts and your minds in Christ Jesus. Finally, brethren, whatever is true, whatever is honorable, whatever is right, whatever is pure, whatever is lovely, whatever is of good report, if there is any excellence or **anything worthy of praise**, let your mind dwell on these things. The things you have learned and received and heard and seen in me, **practice these things**; and the God of peace shall be with you." Phil. 4:6-9.

Clearly most battles are won or lost in the mind. Follow the Lord's advice for peace in the midst of your trials to gain victory over them – PRAISE the Lord in the midst of them! Rejoice for what you KNOW He is doing. Then think on this, speak of this, and listen to only this. Many times close friends call to tell you what your wife is up to. These usually are not "good reports" and most of the time they are not lovely, pure or right – so don't listen!

If you wife has contact with you, don't try to be her friend by listening to all the stuff she is doing with her new boyfriend. Too many men have erroneously thought that this type of "friendship" would win their wives back. For you to pretend that you don't care that she is with someone else, or to "wish her well" when she tells you she is getting married, is sending her the wrong message. She must know she is free to go, but don't lead her to believe that you are happy about it.

Faith is NOT seen. So often men and women write to us because they are looking for signs of improvement in their marriage or in their spouse's attitude toward them. You must remember that Scripture is very clear – faith is **unseen**! When others ask you about your situation, answer them with, "Praise the Lord, God is working!"

"Therefore we do not lose heart, but though our outer man is decaying, yet our inner man is being renewed day by day. For our **momentary light affliction** is producing for us a far more eternal weight in glory far beyond comparison, while we look not at the things which are seen, but the things which are **not seen**, for the things which are seen are **temporal**, but the things which are **not seen are eternal**." 2Cor. 4:16-18.

Faith is…*not* seen. When you are experiencing what Paul calls "light affliction," it may still feel like it is killing you. Remind yourself of the most important truth: these afflictions are meant to be only **momentary**! And these same afflictions are not only temporary but they are producing something wonderful for you – they are getting you ready for a new and wonderful marriage. Remember, the suffering is temporary but the benefits will last an eternity! "Now **faith** is the assurance of things hoped for, the conviction of things NOT **seen**." Heb. 11:1.

Faith – not by sight. Most people start believing when "they begin to see something happening," but this is not faith! "For we walk by faith, **not by sight**." 2Cor. 5:7.

Looking at our circumstances. When Peter looked at *his* circumstances he sank – and you will, too. "And He said 'Come!' And Peter got out of the boat, and walked on the water and came toward Jesus. But **seeing the wind**, he became frightened, and beginning to sink, he cried out, saying, 'Lord save me!' And immediately Jesus stretched out His hand and took hold of him, and said to him, 'O you of little faith, why did you doubt?' " Matt. 14:29-31.

For our testing. Probably the most important lesson when seeking the restoration of our marriages is being able to pass our test – the test of our faith in His Word and not being swayed by emotion (anger or hurt) or false statements made by others. "Consider it all joy, my brethren, when you encounter various trials, knowing that the **testing of your faith** produces endurance. And let **endurance** have its perfect result, that you may be perfect and complete, lacking nothing." Jas. 1:2. When you are perfected and your refining is complete, THEN you will see your wife come back to you!

Tested by fire. "In this you greatly rejoice, even though for a little while, if necessary you have been distressed by various trials, that the proof of your faith, being more precious than gold which is perishable, even though **tested by fire**, may be found to **result in praise** and **glory** and **honor** at the revelation of Jesus Christ." 1Pet. 1:6-7.

So many have failed their test and have continued to walk in the desert as the people of Israel did because they lacked faith. They murmured and complained, which led to rebellion. The proof of your faith, which is a heart full of faith and contentment in your PRESENT circumstances, is more precious than gold.

Keep the faith. Do not turn to another plan when things get tough; do not compromise what you started out to do. Satan is known for bringing new (and wrong) solutions to our trials. Discerning and deciding to stay on the right path is the test we must continue to pass. "I have fought the good fight, I have **finished my course**, I have **kept the faith**; henceforth there is laid up for me a crown of righteousness...." 2Tim 4:7.

If you have been walking with the Lord for some time and have become weary, ask God to send you one other man who will help you not **bend** from your commitment. Once again we invite you to join our ministry to obtain an Encouragement Partner. "Two are better than one for they have a good return for their labor. For if either of them falls, the one will lift up his companion. But woe to the one who falls when there is not another to lift him up. Furthermore, if two lie down together they keep warm, but how can one be warm alone? And if one can overpower him who is alone, two can resist him. **A cord of three is not easily broken.**" Eccl. 4:9-12. Here are some three-cord examples found in the Scriptures:

Moses, Aaron and Hur: "But Moses' hands were heavy. Then they took a stone and put it under him, and he sat on it; and Aaron and Hur supported his hands, one on one side and one on the other. Thus his hands were steady until the sun set." Ex. 17:12. Also see **Shadrach**, **Meshach** and **Abed-nego** in the book of Daniel chapter 3. You, just ONE friend and the Lord are a POWERFUL threefold cord!!

Ask God for guidance through EVERY trial. "Trust in the Lord with all thine heart; and *lean* not unto thine own understanding. In all your ways acknowledge Him and He will direct thy paths." Prov. 3:5-7.

Let us call on **Him** for strength, draw close to **Him** in our time of need. Let us allow **Him** to discipline us, try us, and test us. Let us rejoice always in *all* **things**, not just the good but also the troubles that come our way. Let us keep our hope close to our lips and stay steadfast in our minds. Let us always remember that it is **His will** that we face these hard times and that they are for our good!

"Let us rejoice that He considers us worthy to suffer for His name!" Acts 5:41.

"And we know that **God** causes all things to work together **for good** to those who **love God**, to those who are called according to **His purpose**." Romans 8:28.

Personal commitment: to consider it all joy when I encounter various trials. "Based on what I have learned from God's Word, I commit to allowing the **testing of my faith** to help produce my

endurance. And I will let **endurance** have its perfect result, that I may be perfect and complete, lacking nothing."

Date:_____Signed: _____

A Quick Reference to Trials and Tribulations

God is the One in control, not man and NOT the devil!

1. Justice is from the **Lord**. Prov. 29:26.

2. An answer is from the **Lord**. Prov. 16:1.

3. The heart is turned by the **Lord**. Prov. 21:1.

4. Their deeds are in **God's** hand. Eccl. 9:1.

5. **Thou** (God) has done it. Ps. 44:9-15.

6. **He** (God) raised the storm. Ps. 107:1-32.

7. **He** (God) removed lover and friend. Ps. 88:8,18.

What do our Trials do FOR us?

1. That the power of Christ will dwell in us. 2Cor. 12:9-10.

2. We will learn to be content. Phil. 4:9.

3. We will receive a reward. 2Tim. 4:7,19.

4. We lack nothing. Jas. 1:2-4.

5. He will enable us to comfort others. 2Cor. 3:1-4.

6.   He will perfect what He started in us. Phil. 1:6-13.

7.   We will have our loved one back. Philemon 1:15.

8.   We will receive mercy. Heb. 4:15.

9.   We will learn obedience. Heb. 5:7-8.

10. They will produce endurance. Jas. 1:2-4.

11. We will receive the Crown of Life. Jas. 1:12.

12. We will prove our faith. 1Pet. 1:6-7.

13. We will follow in His steps. 1Pet. 2:21.

14. We will share in His sufferings. 1Pet. 3:13.

Chapter 5

Your First Love

"But I have this against you,
that you have left your first love."
Revelation 2:4

Have you left your first love? Who is your first love? Was your wife your first love? Was it sports or a hobby? Was your job or your career first in your life? Who or what is really **first** in your life? "He who loves father or mother more than Me is not worthy of Me; and he who loves son or daughter more than Me is not worthy of Me." Matt. 10:37. The Scripture in Revelation says: "But I have this against you, that you have left your **first love**." Rev. 2:4.

What is our Lord saying to us? He is saying that any time we put someone or something ahead of our love for or our relationship with Him, then we are not worthy of His Love.

Seek first. You are to put Him first in your priorities, first in your day and first in your heart. "But **seek first** His kingdom and His righteousness; and all these things shall be added unto you." Matt. 6:33. When, if ever, has the Lord been first in your life?

Dirty rags. Ask yourself these questions: Do the things I put first have eternal value? Will what I do today help to increase His kingdom? Am I seeking after His righteousness or trying to muster up my own righteousness? Remember, our righteousness is like **dirty rags**! (Is. 64:6.)

What happens when you put someone ahead of the Lord? What does He do to draw you back to Him? If you have put your wife ahead of your love for the Lord, then it was the Lord who has taken your wife from you. "**Thou** hast removed my acquaintances far from me; **Thou** hast made me an object of loathing to them. Thou has removed lover and friend far from me; my acquaintances are in darkness." Ps. 88:8,18. And don't make marriage restoration first in your life; you *must* make the Lord first in your life!

"If You Love Me...Obey"

After you put God first in your life, you must then cast down the false doctrine that says "you are saved by grace, so it's really OKAY to sin, because we are no longer under the Law." Let's search the Scriptures:

Do your deeds deny Him? "They profess to know God, but their **deeds deny Him**, being detestable and disobedient and worthless for any good deed." Titus 1:16.

Do you do what His Word says? "Why do you call Me, Lord, and do not do what I say?" Luke 6:46.

Are we to continue in sin? "What shall we say then? **Are we to continue in sin** that grace might increase? May it never be! How shall we who died to sin still live in it?" "What then? Shall we sin because we are not under law but under grace? May it never be!" Rom. 6:1-2,15.

Faith without works is dead. "What use is it, my brethren, if a man says he has faith, but he has no works? Can that faith save him?" "For just as the body without the spirit is dead, so also **faith without works is dead**." Jas. 2:14,26. Good works are the "fruits" of our salvation. These are the questions we must ask ourselves:

Do my deeds deny that I follow the Lord?

Does grace give me a license to sin?

Am I, as a believer, to produce good works?

I never knew you. Many believe that you can live any way you wish and then enter into heaven once you die. Is this true? "Many will say to Me on that day, 'Lord, Lord, did we not prophesy in Your name, and in Your name cast out demons, and in Your name perform many miracles?' And then I will declare to them, '**I never knew you**; depart from me, you who practice lawlessness.' " Matt. 7:22-23. The answer then is "no!"

Confess your sins. If this is the mind that you had, prior to learning these Scriptures, do as Scripture says: "Therefore, **confess your sins** one to another, and pray for one another, so that you may be healed." Jas. 5:16

Obedience to His Word

"**Wisdom** shouts in the street, she lifts her voice in the square. At the head of the noisy streets she cries out; at the entrance to the gate in the city, she utters her sayings, how long, O naive ones, will you love simplicity. And scoffers delight themselves in scoffing, and fools hate knowledge. **Turn to my reproof**, behold, **I will pour out my spirit on you**; I will make my words known to you.

"Because I called and you refused; I stretched out my hand, and no one paid attention; and you neglected all my counsel, and did not want my reproof; **I will even laugh at your calamity; I will mock when your dread comes**, when your dread comes on like a storm, and your calamity comes on like a whirlwind, when distress and anguish come on you.

"Then they will call on me but I will not answer; they will seek me diligently, but they will not find me, **because they hated knowledge, and did not choose the fear of the Lord**. They would not accept my counsel, they spurned all my reproof. So they shall eat of the fruit of their own way, and be satiated with their own devices. For the waywardness of the naive shall kill them, and the complacency of fools shall destroy them. **But he who listens to me shall live securely, and shall be at ease from the dread of evil.**" Prov. 1:20-33. Seek wisdom!

Obedience comes from the *heart*. "…you became obedient from the **heart** to that form of teaching to which you were committed." Rom. 6:17. And again, "for God sees not as man sees, for man looks at the outward appearance, but the Lord looks at the heart." 1Sam 16:7.

Obedience needs *testing*. "Do not be surprised at the fiery trial which comes upon you for your **testing**." 1Pet. 4:12. Obedience *purifies* your soul. "Since you have in obedience to the truth **purified your souls**…." 1Pet. 1:22.

Obedience gives *testimony* of who your Father is. "Obey My voice and I will be your God, and you will be My people; and you will walk in all the way in which I command you, that it may be well with you. Yet they did not obey or incline their ear, but walked in their own counsels and in the stubbornness of their evil heart, and went backward and not forward." Jer. 7:23-24.

Your disobedience actually praises the wicked. "Those who forsake the law PRAISE **the wicked**, but those who keep the law strive with them." Prov. 28:4. The prayers of the disobedient go unheard. "He who turns away his ear from listening to the law, even his prayer is an abomination." Prov. 28:9.

Our Example of Obedience Is Jesus

He was obedient *even unto death*. "He humbled Himself by becoming obedient to the point of death, even death on a cross." Phil. 2:5-11. "Although He was a Son, He *learned obedience* from the things which He suffered." Heb. 5:7-10. Could it be said of you that you, too, are learning obedience through the sufferings that you are experiencing?

He was obedient and submissive to His authority. "My Father, if it is possible, let this cup pass from Me; yet **not as I will**, but Thou wilt. My Father, if this cannot pass away unless I drink it, **Thy will be done**." Matt. 26:39, 42.

Are you in submission to your authority? "But I want you to understand that Christ is the head of every man, and the man is the head of a woman, and God is the head of Christ." 1Cor. 11:3. If you are like many Christian men, you are quick to point out your wife's lack of submissiveness to you. But are you setting a good example of submissiveness to your authority, which is Christ? Do you follow and seek Him? Do you follow after His commands in tithing, leading your family spiritually and in the way you treat (or treated) your wife (as the weaker vessel, in an understanding way)?

The secret to success. "All the paths of the Lord are **lovingkindness** and truth to those *who keep His covenant and His testimonies.* For Thy name's sake, O Lord, pardon my iniquity, for it is great. Who is the man who fears the Lord? He will instruct him in the way he should choose. His soul will abide in prosperity, and his descendants will inherit the land. The **secret of the Lord** is for **those who fear Him**." Ps. 25:10-15. The only way to treat your wife with the lovingkindness due her is to fear the Lord. This is the secret that so few men know. For if a man has a true and genuine fear of God, then he is a true follower of the Word and of Christ.

Self-condemned. Unfortunately, most men dispute or argue the true meaning of the Scriptures -- missing the blessings of a life wholly devoted to the Lord. "But shun foolish controversies and genealogies and strife and disputes about the Law; for they are unprofitable and worthless. Reject a factious man after a first and second warning, knowing that such a man is perverted and is sinning, being **self-condemned**." Titus 3:9-11.

Turn aside to myths. Instead of searching for the truth, many want others to agree with their wrong ideas or decisions: "But wanting to have their ears tickled, they will accumulate for themselves teachers in accordance to their own desires; and will **turn aside to myths**." 2Tim. 4:3-4.

Obedience to His Word. "Do not be as the horse or as the mule which have no understanding, whose trappings include bit and bridle to hold them in check, otherwise they will not come near to you." Ps. 32:9. If you don't obey His commandments in your daily pursuits and in your dealings with your wife, He will discipline you. "The Lord has **disciplined me** severely, but He has not given me over to death. I shall not die but live, and tell of the works of the Lord." Ps. 118:18,17. Don't waste your time looking at your wife's faults and blaming her for your marriage troubles, it is YOU He is disciplining, by turning your wife's heart away from you. This is the reason for her indifference to you.

God is faithful to His Word. "If his sons forsake My law, and do not walk in My judgments, If they violate My statutes, and do not keep My commandments, then I will visit their transgressions with a rod, and their iniquity with stripes." Ps. 89:30-34. If you continue in rebellion to God's Word or your authority, Jesus Christ, who was meek and lowly, then God will continue to punish you.

Keep your Eyes Focused on the Lord

Whom do you want to please? You are to try and please *the **Lord**, rather than your wife or anyone else in your life. "When a man's ways are pleasing to the LORD, He makes even his enemies to be at peace with him." Prov. 16:7. "Delight yourself in the LORD; And He will give you the desires of your heart." Prov. 31:3.

The truth is, when you do what is right by the Lord's standards, you will see your wife's heart turning back to you. However, if don't begin to notice a more peaceful atmosphere when conversing with your wife, then you are either still preoccupied and obsessed with her, or you are harboring a self-righteous spirit.

Why not *try* and please my wife? That was man's first mistake. Let's look at some scriptural facts. "When the woman saw that the tree was good for food, and that it was a delight to the eyes, and that the tree was desirable to make one wise, she took from its fruit and ate; and **she gave** also to her husband *with her*, and he ate." Gen. 3:6. Why would Adam eat the fruit when he knew it was wrong?

Man sinned knowingly. It's important to note that *the woman was not created* until Gen. 2:22, five verses later. We never see God commanding Eve directly. The point is that Eve was deceived. Adam knowingly sinned.

Woman was created for man. God gave Adam dominion over all living things in the garden, including Eve. Eve was created for Adam, not the other way around. "...for indeed man was not created for the woman's sake, but woman for the man's sake." 1Cor. 11:9. "Then the LORD God said, 'It is not good for the man to be alone; I will make him a helper suitable for him.' " Gen. 2:18.

Adam never stopped Eve, though he *was* **with** her. "...and *she gave* also to her husband *with her*, and he ate." Gen. 3:6. Why? Why did he also eat it? Is it possible that Adam was trying to please his wife?

Why didn't he stop her? Did he just want to let her do what she wanted even though in his heart he knew it was a mistake? What about you? Do you do things just to please your wife, not even considering what God thinks about it? Have you many times let your wife (or your children) do things that in your heart you knew was a mistake? The consequences may be that now she is in deep sin and out from under your protection and authority.

However, do not allow this truth to make you puffed up as one who is superior so that an attitude of control and aggressiveness should take over. This insight should bring you to a place of humility as you reflect upon how you have failed to lead and protect your wife and now find yourself in the situation you are in today.

What does Adam do when things go wrong? When confronted by God after he sinned, what does Adam do? "And the man said, 'The woman whom Thou gavest to be with me, she gave me from the tree, and I ate.' " Gen. 3:12. He blames Eve. It was her fault! The bottom line is that he also blames God! Well, there is no doubt Eve was wrong to eat the fruit. But why isn't she blamed for the fall of man if she ate it first and then gave it to Adam? Why is sin not passed down through her?

"Therefore, just as through *one man sin entered into the world*, and death through sin, and so death spread to all men, because all sinned…" Rom. 5:12. In the same way it was through YOUR sin, that sin entered *your* house. Was it your sin of anger? Was it your sin of neglect? Or was it your sin of self-indulgence? If you had been the proper husband, spiritual leader, and man of lovingkindness you should have been, do you think you would you be in the position you are in today?

Eve was deceived, but Adam knew. Adam was ultimately responsible and accountable before God for the sin committed, not Eve. "Then to Adam He said, 'Because you have *listened to the voice of your wife*, and have eaten from the tree about *which I commanded you*, saying, 'You shall not eat from it….' " Gen. 3:17. As men, we are the ones who are ultimately responsible for our marriages and families.

It doesn't matter what your wife is doing now or what she has done in the past; you must take responsibility. It is crucial that you embrace this mindset and turn your eyes of blame totally inward; for only then will you begin to become a godly man and regain your wife's love and trust.

You are your wife's protector. Men, God put us over our wives for their protection, not so we can control, intimidate, or use them for our pleasure! The woman was deceived; therefore, God knew she was susceptible to Satan's deceptive schemes. Therefore, He assigned man to rule over her. "To the woman He said, 'I will greatly multiply your pain in childbirth, *in pain* you shall bring forth children; [*pain in childbirth was her curse*] Yet your desire shall be for your husband, and he shall rule over you.' " Gen. 3:16. Also, as we can see, woman's punishment was not that she would bear children; it was that she would have *pain* when they were brought forth.

Nor was her curse to have her husband rule over her as the feminists would have us to believe. However, when a husband does not demonstrate a Christ-like love for his wife or he allows sin to get a stronghold in his life, then he can become like a curse to his wife.

"And it was *not Adam* who was **deceived**, but the *woman* being *quite* **deceived**, fell into transgression." 1Tim. 2:14. Have you neglected to protect your wife? Have you left her totally open to deception due to your ill treatment of her? If so, repent!

But don't make the mistake of telling her that she is being deceived. When a person really is deceived they can no longer discern right from wrong. Confronting her will only drive her farther away from you and from God. At this point, your time would be best spent finding out how to become a godly man and husband. Much can be learned by reading the manual for men, *A Wise Man Builds Upon A Rock*, available for free to read on our website, or to order a copy. Then use prayer to protect your wife and to change the situation she is in.

Spiritual Protection

Women in the church. "Let the *women* keep silent in the churches; for they are not permitted to speak, but let them subject themselves, just as the Law also says. And if they desire to *learn anything*, let them ask their **own husbands** at home; for it is improper for a woman to speak in church." 1Cor. 14:34-35. Why do churches and Christian seminars seem to attract more women than men? It is primarily because women have a deep craving for spiritual things and their husbands are not meeting their obligation to help fulfill this need.

Aren't we as men supposed to be the leaders? If men are missing from the church and from the spiritual things pertaining to the family, then are we *really* leading our families?

Are you capable of answering your wife's spiritual questions? Maybe your wife is not asking you any questions because of the poor example you have set as a Christian leader. Are you as well versed in the Bible as your wife is? Have you taken the same amount of time seeking the things of God as you have in seeking other things that interest you?

Captivating weak women. "For among them are those who enter into households and *captivate* **weak women** weighed down with sins, led on by various impulses, **always learning** and never able to come to the knowledge of the truth." 2Tim. 3:6. Certainly, there are things your wife needs to learn from another – an older woman, such as the things found in the book of Titus – but what have you taught her by your example?

Weak women? Are you aware that in God's Word it says in 1Pet. 3:7, "You husbands likewise, live with your wives in an *understanding* way, as with a **weaker vessel**, *since she is a woman....*" Have you treated your wife as a weaker vessel or have you treated her with harshness and hardheartedness? God's Word says that we as men are to live with our wives differently, in an understanding way, as with a weaker vessel, since she is a woman. Have you taken the time to really listen to your wife share her thoughts and concerns from her heart? Or has she stopped opening up her heart to you because what she has said has fallen on a deaf ear? An ear so embittered that no kindness, sympathy or understanding would be the response to her deep and wounded cry?

Honor her as a fellow heir. Have you treated your wife as a lower class citizen in the Kingdom of God? Have you acted arrogantly as the leader of your home? Then you need to read the entire verse that we have been referring to. "You husbands likewise, live with your wives in an understanding way, as with a weaker vessel, since she is a woman; and grant her *honor* as a fellow heir of the grace of life, so that your prayers may not be hindered." 1Pet. 3:7. God is so adamant about how a husband is to treat his wife that he assigns a punishment for a husband who fails to treat his wife appropriately -- your prayers will be hindered. Have your prayers recently been answered? If not, then it is time to take a serious look at your relationship with your wife.

The fact is, the fate of your entire household rests on you. Do not attempt to take the speck out of your wife's eye and concentrate on her shortcomings. If you were a patient, kind and understanding husband like you should be with your wife, she would turn back to you in an instant. God created her with a desire for you! It says in

Gen. 3:16, God speaking to the wife, "...your desire shall be for your husband..." Your wife was created with a longing to be with you. However, if she is treated harshly instead of in "an understanding way, as with a weaker vessel, since she is a woman" then you will see her heart's desire for you die; making her vulnerable to the affections of another.

It's time to pray Psalm 51 aloud:

"Wash me thoroughly from my iniquity, and cleanse me from my sin. For I know my transgressions, and my sin is ever before me. Against Thee, Thee only, have I sinned, and done what is evil in Thy sight. Create in me a clean heart, O God, and renew a steadfast spirit within me. Do not take Thy Holy Spirit from me. Restore to me the joy of Thy salvation, and sustain me with a willing spirit. Then I will teach transgressors Thy ways, and sinners will be converted to Thee. The sacrifices of God are a broken spirit; a broken and contrite heart, O God, Thou will not despise."

May God be with you as you strive to be more like Christ!

Personal commitment: to put the Lord first in my life. "Based on what I have learned in Scripture, I commit to do everything as unto the Lord. I will show the Lord my commitment to Him and my obedience to His Word by submitting to those who are in authority over me, especially my Lord and Savior, Jesus Christ, by following His example. I will treat my wife as a weaker vessel, in an understanding way, since she is a woman, and grant her honor as a fellow heir, rather than a second class citizen, so that my prayers will no longer be hindered."

Date:_____Signed: _____

Chapter 6

The Angry Man

"He who is slow to anger
is better than the mighty,
And he who rules his spirit,
than he who captures a city."
Proverbs 16:32.

Ask yourself, "Am I an angry man?"

If you answered "no," what if someone asked your wife, your children, or those you work with if you are an angry man, would they also say "no"? Anger is mentioned 266 times in the Bible. Most of those references are to God's anger towards those who sin repeatedly without repenting. Using the verse in Eph. 4:26, we have heard preacher say that we are *commanded* to be angry. Is this true? Let's search His Word for the wisdom of God regarding anger.

Angry Men

Angry Cain. There are many accounts in Scripture of angry men and the consequences suffered by those who could not master their anger. These men kept trying to "rise above" their anger. Satan deceived them, because to master anger you must first *bow down* with humility. "...but for Cain and for his offering He had no regard. So Cain became **very angry** and his countenance fell. Then the LORD said to Cain, 'Why are you angry? And why has your countenance fallen? If you do well, will not your countenance be lifted up? And if you do not do well, sin is crouching at the door; and its desire is for you, but you must master it.' " Gen. 4:5. It was Cain's pride that made him envy and become angry with his brother.

Moses

Angry Moses. Moses was a man whom God used mightily; yet, it was his anger that often got in his way. "But they did not listen to Moses...and Moses was angry with them." Exod. 16:20. Many times he was angry due to the disobedience and sinfulness of those whom he was to lead to the Promised Land. Do you ever get angry with those whom you have been assigned to lead? "An angry man stirs up strife, and a hot-tempered man abounds in transgression." Prov. 29:22.

"But **Moses**...was **angry** with Aaron's surviving sons." Lev. 10:16.

"Then **Moses** became **very angry** and said to the LORD, 'Do not regard their offering! I have not taken a single donkey from them, nor have I done harm to any of them.' " Num. 16:15.

"And **Moses** was **angry** with the officers of the army." Num. 31:14.

"And it came about, as soon as **Moses** came near the camp, that he saw the calf and the dancing; and Moses' **anger burned**, and *he threw* the tablets from his hands and shattered them at the foot of the mountain." Exod. 32:19.

Men, have you ever thrown anything when you were angry? Don't make the mistake of using Moses' anger as an excuse for your own anger. The truth is that God *did* use him mightily *in spite of* his weakness in this area, but for you to excuse sin in your life would be placing yourself on dangerous ground.

Slaves of sin. Are **you a slave of sin**? "Do you not know that when you present yourselves to someone as slaves for obedience, you are slaves of the one whom you obey, either of sin resulting in death, or of obedience resulting in righteousness?" Rom. 6:16.

Yes, Moses was used mightily, but his anger ultimately caused him to miss the blessing of going into the Promised Land.

We shall all stand. Is anger the only sin in your life, or are there other sins such as immorality, coveting, drunkenness, or carousing? "But you, why do you judge your brother? Or you again, why do you regard your brother with contempt? For **we shall all stand** before the judgment seat of God." Rom. 14:10.

Jonah

Angry Jonah. "But it greatly displeased **Jonah**, and **he became angry**." Jonah 4:1. "And the LORD said (to Jonah), 'Do you have good reason to be **angry**?' " Jonah 4:4. After you calm down, aren't you often surprised when you realize how stupid it was to get so angry over something so small and insignificant?

"Then God said to Jonah, 'Do you have good reason to be **angry** about the plant?' And he said, 'I have *good reason* to be **angry**, even to death.'" Jonah 4:9. Have you ever had good reason to be angry — angry at your wife, angry with your children, angry about work?

What did Jesus say about being angry? "But I say to you that *everyone* who is **angry** with his brother shall be guilty before the court; and whoever shall say to his brother, 'Raca,' shall be guilty before the Supreme Court; and whoever shall say, 'You fool,' shall be guilty enough to go into the fiery hell." Matt. 5:22. Was Jesus just talking about anger with a brother? No. He was talking about being angry with *anyone*, even your wife or your children. Does that mean that anger can cause us to be guilty enough for hell? Yes, it does. But as Christians, if we repent, Christ saves us from the consequences of our sins.

"*If we confess* our sins, He is faithful and righteous to forgive us our sins and to cleanse us from all unrighteousness." 1John 1:9. The verse says "if" we confess. The question then is, have you confessed this sin of anger to the Lord *your* Savior? Have you confessed it to those whom you have offended? "Raca" is a word that means "worthless" in Greek. Have you ever told your wife or children, in so many words, that they were worthless? Then you are guilty of fiery hell, unless you repent. If you think that you will lose their respect by asking them to forgive you, try it and see. They may just give you the respect that you've desired from them for a long time.

Angry tempers. "For I am afraid that perhaps when I come I may find you to be not what I wish and may be found by you to be not what you wish; that perhaps there may be strife, jealousy, **angry tempers**, disputes, slanders, gossip, arrogance, disturbances...." 2Cor. 12:20. What would your brothers in Christ find if they walked into *your* home or office unannounced?

Commanded to be angry? As we said, we have heard preachers have use the following verse to tell those who want to have their ears tickled that we are actually *commanded* to be angry. Taken out of context this would seem true. Yet, when searching for the truth, you need only read the entire verse. "Be angry and yet do not sin; **do not let the sun go down on your anger** and **do not give the devil an opportunity**...Let no unwholesome word proceed from your mouth, but only such a word as is good for edification according to the need of the moment, that it may give grace to those who hear...And **do not grieve the Holy Spirit** of God...Let all bitterness and wrath and **anger** and clamor and slander **be put away from you**, along with all malice. And **be kind to one another, tender-hearted, forgiving each other**, just as God in Christ also has forgiven you." Eph. 4:26-32. Anger is a natural reaction when someone offends us, or should we say a *fleshly reaction*. But as followers of Christ, we are asked to walk in the Spirit! "But I say, walk by the Spirit, and you will not carry out the desire of the flesh." Gal. 5:16.

Walk in love. "Therefore be imitators of God, as beloved children; and **walk in love**, just as Christ also loved you, and gave Himself up for us, an offering and a sacrifice to God as a fragrant aroma." Eph. 5:1.

Family scattered. "Cursed be their **anger**, for it is fierce; and their wrath, for it is cruel. I will disperse them in Jacob, and scatter them in Israel." Gen. 49:7. Has your family been scattered? Do your children go outside or play with friends because they are fearful of your anger when you are home? Are your teens or young adults gone because of your anger? "And, **fathers, do not provoke your children to anger**; but bring them up in the discipline and instruction of the Lord." Eph. 6:4.

Slow to Anger

God tells us that He is slow to anger. "Then the LORD passed by in front of him and proclaimed, 'The LORD, the LORD God, compassionate and gracious, **slow to anger**, and **abounding in lovingkindness** and truth....' " Num. 14:18. "The LORD is gracious and merciful; **slow to anger** and **great in lovingkindness**." Ps. 145:8.

Are you slow or quick to anger? God describes the difference between a man who follows God and one who does not. "He who is **slow to anger** has great understanding, but he who is **quick-tempered exalts folly**." Prov. 14:29. Do you exalt folly? If you are quick tempered, you do.

Do you stir up strife, or do you calm contentions? "A hot-tempered man stirs up strife, but the **slow to anger** pacifies contention." Prov. 15:18.

Are you better than the mighty? "He who is **slow to anger** is **better than the mighty**, and he who rules his spirit, than he who captures a city." Prov. 16:32.

The anger of man does not achieve the righteousness of God. "This you know, my beloved brethren. But let everyone be quick to hear, slow to speak and slow to anger; for the anger of man does not achieve the righteousness of God." James 1:19.

How to Gain Control of Your Anger

Practice discretion. "A man's **discretion** makes him **slow to anger**, and it is his glory to overlook a transgression." Prov.

19:11. How do you gain discretion? "I, **wisdom**, dwell with prudence, and I find knowledge and **discretion**." Prov. 8:12.

Obtain wisdom. "Scorners set a city aflame, but **wise men** *turn away* **anger**." Prov. 29:8. Where do you find wisdom? In fearing the LORD. "The **fear of the LORD** is the beginning of **wisdom**...." Ps. 111:10. "The **fear of the LORD** is the beginning of **wisdom**...." Prov. 9:10.

There is nothing anyone can do to control an angry man. "A man of great anger shall bear the penalty, for if you rescue him, you will only have to do it again." Prov. 19:19.

Is this you in your home? "The **terror** of a king is like the growling of a lion; he who provokes him to **anger** *forfeits his own life*." Prov. 20:2.

Anger produces strife. "For the churning of milk produces butter, and pressing the nose brings forth blood; so the churning of **anger** produces strife." Prov. 30:33. Is anger constantly churning inside you? Is everyone expected to walk on eggshells because you may blow up any minute? "Better is a dry morsel and quietness with it than a house full of feasting with **strife**." Prov. 17:1.

Are you "practicing" the deeds of the flesh or fruits of the Spirit? "Now the **deeds of the flesh** *are evident*, which are: immorality, impurity, sensuality, idolatry, sorcery, enmities, **strife**, jealousy, **outbursts of anger**, disputes, dissensions, factions, envying, drunkenness, carousing, and things like these, of which I forewarn you just as I have forewarned you that **those who practice such things shall not inherit the kingdom of God**. But the fruit of the Spirit is love, joy, peace, patience, kindness, goodness, faithfulness, gentleness, self-control; against such things there is no law." Gal. 5:19-23.

Do you practice the fruits of the Spirit, or do you spend your time practicing your anger? "Not everyone who says to Me, 'Lord, Lord,' will enter the kingdom of heaven; but he who does the will of My Father who is in heaven. Many will say to Me on that day, 'Lord,

Lord, did we not prophesy in Your name, and in Your name cast out demons, and in Your name perform many miracles?' And then I will declare to them, 'I never knew you; depart from Me, you who practice lawlessness.' " Matt. 7:21.

Quarrelsome Spirit

Do you have a quarrelsome spirit? "But refuse foolish and ignorant speculations, knowing they produce quarrels. And the Lord's bond-servant **must not be quarrelsome** but be kind to all, able to teach, patient when wronged." 2Tim. 2:23. Are you a "know-it-all"? Or do you have a contrary comment for many of the things others say? God tells us to "Agree with thine adversary quickly while thou art in the way with him, lest at any time thine adversary deliver thee to the judge." Matt. 5:25, KJV. **Watch out for the divorce court!**

Are you argumentative? "Urge bondslaves to be subject to their own masters in everything, to be well- pleasing, **not argumentative**." Titus 2:9. As Jesus' bondslave, you owe it to *Him* to be well-pleasing.

Is there strife in your home? Again, "Better is a dry morsel and quietness with it than a house full of feasting and strife." Prov. 17:1. Are your children loud and unruly? Help keep your children quiet; it's not just your wife's job. (For more knowledge, read the lesson "Father's Instructions" in *A Wise Man Manual for Men*, for "My people are destroyed for a lack of knowledge." Hosea 4:6.)

Do you ever quarrel with your wife? "The beginning of strife is like letting out of water, so abandon the **quarrel** before it breaks out." Prov. 17:14. Many so-called "marriage experts" tell us that a good fight is actually healthy for a marriage. **Don't you believe it!**

Was I Not Joking?

Are you a madman? Do you tease your wife about her weaknesses or sometimes about things which she has confided in you? "Like a

madman who throws firebrands, arrows and death, so is the man who deceives his neighbor [or his wife], and says, '*Was I not joking?*' " Prov. 26:18-19.

Empty words, silly talk, or coarse jesting. "But do not let immorality or any impurity or greed even be named among you, as is proper among saints; and there must be no filthiness and **silly talk**, or **coarse jesting**, which are not fitting, but rather giving of thanks. For this you know with certainty, that no immoral or impure person or covetous man, who is an idolater, has an inheritance in the kingdom of Christ and God. Let no one deceive you with **empty words**, for because of these things the wrath of God comes upon the sons of disobedience."

"Therefore **do not be partakers with them**; for you were formerly darkness, but now you are light in the Lord; walk as children of light (for the fruit of the light consists in all goodness and righteousness and truth), trying to learn what is pleasing to the Lord. And do not participate in the unfruitful deeds of darkness, but instead even expose them; for it is disgraceful even to speak of the things which are done by them in secret. But all things become visible when they are exposed by the light, for everything that becomes visible is light." Eph. 5:3-13.

Speak as a child. Most women hate to be teased. Some are good sports about it; most are not. As boys, we may have teased the outcasts at school or our brothers and sisters. "When I was a child, I used to **speak as a child**, think as a child, reason as a child; when I became a man, I did away with childish things." 1Cor. 13:11. As men, we must put away our childish ways.

Slanderer. Never expose to others a weakness in your wife, nor tell others something your wife has told you in confidence. "**A slanderer separates intimate friends.**" Prov. 16:28.

Others may think we're funny, but God knows our heart. "Whoever secretly **slanders** his neighbor, him I will destroy." Ps. 101:5. "It is a terrifying thing to fall into the hands of the living God." Hebr. 10:31.

Let's all put this type of talk away from us. "Let all bitterness and wrath and anger and clamor and **slander** be put away from you, along with all malice." Eph. 4:31.

The Source of Your Anger...Pride!

"Now I, Nebuchadnezzar, praise, exalt, and honor the King of heaven, for all *His* works are true and *His* ways just, and *He* is able to **humble those who walk in pride**." Daniel 5:37.

Why are so many men angry? Is it because Christian men often imitate the world and the world's thinking? In far too many cases, the books we read, the counselors we seek and the classes we attend do not reflect God's Word. We are instead presented with a "Christianized" worldly view.

God's Word is pure and uncompromising.

Poison dipped in chocolate is still poison! Men, the deadly, worldly views are more dangerous when they are dipped in Christianity because we eat it right up! We have been deceived into thinking that "self-love" and "self-esteem" are good things; yet, these attitudes are the root of many of our problems.

It's the "know-it-all" who argues and wants his own way, because he knows (actually thinks) he is right. And when he is wrong, his self-esteem needs to be protected. There is never a humble word or an "I'm sorry." The angry man has been conditioned to think that to make an apology would be too humiliating a sign of weakness. His "self-love" will train him to continue to climb up on his pedestal of pride, only to fall again and again.

What is the cure? "And when they came to Marah, they could not drink the waters of Marah, for they were bitter; therefore it was named Marah." Exodus 15:23. Moses threw a tree into the water, a representation of the cross of Calvary. You must also throw the Cross into your sea of bitterness. Christ died to free you from all sin, including anger, pride, and self-absorbed behavior.

Here is God's prescription. God told us that if we as a nation would **humble ourselves**, seek His face and turn from our wicked ways, He would heal our land. Instead, we "walk in the counsel of the wicked" (Ps. 1:1) and we "trust in mankind" (Jer. 17:5). This is why we have superficial healing! "The brokenness of His people is healed superficially." Jer. 8:11.

Look at all the psychology in the church. What does psychology (straw) have in common with God's Word (grain)? "'The prophet who has a dream may relate his dream, but let him who has My Word speak My Word in truth. What does straw have in common with grain?' declares the Lord. 'Behold, I am against the prophets,' declares the Lord, 'who use their tongues and declare, 'the Lord declares.'" Jer. 23:28, 31. It is extremely dangerous for Christians to act as if man's ideas or psychology is God's Word, or to use God's Word to promote current worldly views.

Self-esteem

Are you training and encouraging your children to have "self-esteem"? The word self-esteem is all too often acceptable word used by parents; however, it is just another word for "pride." Remember, it's a wolves' word in sheep's clothing! You will soon see your child act arrogant and self-absorbed. What child needs to be built up to feel good about himself? From birth, a child wants his own way and is completely self-absorbed!

Building self-esteem. There are books and books and more books written for Christians, by Christians, but many of the teachings *do not* represent what God teaches in His Word. Let's look at what God tells us about "building our self-esteem" or "building our child's self-esteem." Let's find out why we should be careful *not to say*, "I have my *pride!*" or "I am so *proud* of you" but instead say things in "all humility" (Eph. 4:2).

Pride is a sin. Pride was the sin committed by the angel Lucifer, who later became Satan. "Your heart was lifted up because of your beauty; you corrupted your wisdom by reason of your splendor. I

(God) cast you to the ground." Ezek. 28:17. Satan also said, "I will make myself like the Most High." Isaiah 14:14.

"Self-esteem" began as a lie, formed by twisting Scripture. Satan used Scripture when he tempted Jesus in the desert; he still uses it today. He just twists it a little, making it a half-truth. But we know that anything that is half true is a lie, lest we forget Abraham and Sarah ("she is my sister").

"Love your neighbor as yourself." Matt. 22:39. Those who have degrees in psychology will often try and convince you that this means you have to love yourself before you can love anyone else. In other words, "self-love" is needed first because some of us, or most of us, hate ourselves. Is this the truth or a lie? It is a lie because it contradicts God's Word. "For **no one EVER hated his own flesh**, but nourishes and cherishes it." Eph. 5:29.

Jesus teaches that if we are *humble* we will be blessed. "Blessed are the humble [gentle, meek] for they shall inherit the earth." Matt. 5:5. We are to think of others as more important than ourselves.

Those who contemplate or threaten suicide are often told by the world that they hate themselves, but that contradicts the Word of God. Remember, God said that "*no one* ever hated his own flesh"! Satan tries to blind people with pain until they are not thinking clearly.

What is the root cause of their pain or the spirit that is overwhelming them? Is it a spirit of depression or a spirit of oppression? If there is a "spirit of death" in your home, see if this sin has been passed down from a family member. A person who threatens suicide is crying out for help. Help them by giving them love and comfort; share the truth. Once they are out of the woods, encourage them to pray in thanksgiving, thanking God for *everything*, including the trials, "knowing they are working together for good." Rom. 8:28.

"Do nothing from selfishness or empty conceit, but with *humility of mind* let each of you regard one another as more important than himself; do not merely look out for your own personal interests, but also for the interests of others." Phil. 2:3.

The world tells us to speak well of ourselves, but Jesus said, "And whoever exalts himself shall be humbled; and whoever humbles himself shall be exalted." Matt. 23:12.

Learn from Nebuchadnezzar – his grandson didn't! We read that Nebuchadnezzar, who was proud of his power and wealth, was made to be like the cattle and eat grass. Yet, his grandson chose to exalt himself: "Yet you, his son, Belshazzar, have not **humbled** your heart, even though you knew all this, but you have exalted yourself." Dan. 5:22-23.

Pride is evil: it will cause God to humble you. You may think that certain things you go through are humiliating, but God means them for your good. He doesn't want to humiliate you; He wants to humble you.

Pride is not of God. "For from within, out of the heart of men proceed the evil...pride." Mark 7:21. "For all that is in the world, the lust of the flesh, and the lust of the eyes and the **boastful pride of life**, is not of the Father, but is from the world." 1John 2:16. Pride is not of God!

Why do you boast? "For who regards you as superior? And what do you have that you did not receive? But if you did receive it, why do you boast?" 1Cor. 4:7. "For everyone who exalts himself shall be humbled, and he who humbles himself shall be exalted." Luke 14:11. If we tell others to speak highly of themselves, we are only setting a net for their feet! "...unwilling to lift up his eyes to heaven...for everyone who exalts himself shall be humbled, but he who humbles himself shall be exalted." Luke 18:14. We have often heard, "Stand tall and be proud!" Instead, we must learn to die to self.

Die to your "self." "For you have died and your life is hidden with Christ in God." Col. 3:3. "...and He died for all, that they who live should no longer live for themselves, but for Him who died and rose again on their behalf." 2Cor. 5:15.

Let him deny himself. "But He turned and said to Peter, 'Get behind Me, Satan! You are a stumbling block to Me; for you are not setting your mind on God's interests, but man's.' Then Jesus said to His disciples, 'If anyone wishes to come after Me, let him **deny himself**, and take up his cross, and follow Me. For whoever wishes to save his life shall lose it; but whoever loses his life for My sake shall find it.' " Matt. 16:23.

Do you act as though it is *your* life when there is conflict in your home? Is your wife bothering you? Are your children standing in the way of *your* greatness, wrecking *your* pleasure?

If you are a Christian, you were bought with a price. Your life is not your own. You are on this earth to serve God. Since God blessed you with a wife, you are commanded to love her. To love her, you must put her needs before your own. Have you been blessed with children? If so, then God says you are to train them. Are you training them in the ways of God? Are you training them to be Godly adults, or are you training them to follow the ways of the world? Do they see, by your example, that many other things are more important than God in your life – sports, reading the paper, movies, or work?

Paul was a good example of how we can put Christ first. "For me to live is Christ, and to die is gain." Phil.1:21.

As we humble ourselves, then God is free to exalt us. "Clothe yourselves with *humility* toward one another, for God is opposed to the proud, but *gives grace to the humble. Humble* yourselves, therefore, under the mighty hand of God, that *He* may exalt you at the proper time." 1Pet. 5:5-6. "God is opposed to the proud, but gives grace to the *humble...Humble* yourselves in the presence of the Lord, and *He* will exalt you." James 4:6, 11. "I can do all things *through Christ* who strengthens me." Phil. 4:13. Exalt Christ and others above yourself.

Jesus should be our example, always, in all things, in the way He walked on this earth. "Have this attitude (humility) in yourselves which was also in Christ Jesus, who, although He existed in the form of God, did not regard equality with God a thing to be grasped, but *emptied Himself,* taking the form of a bond-servant, and being made in the likeness of men. And being found in appearance as a man, He *humbled* Himself by becoming obedient to the point of death, even death on a cross. Therefore also God highly exalted Him and bestowed on Him the name which is above every name." Phil 2:5-9.

Daniel also. "...for from the first day that you set your heart on understanding this and on *humbling* yourself before your God, your words were heard." Dan. 10:12.

To Remove Pride

"Take My yoke upon you, and learn from Me, for I am gentle and humble in heart." Matt. 11:29. "But he who boasts, let him **boast in the Lord**. For not he who commends himself is approved, but **whom the Lord commends**." 2Cor 10:17-18. "Let another praise you and **not your own mouth**; a stranger and not your own lips." Prov. 27:2. Practice using the word "pleased" as a substitute for the word "proud."

And if you don't humble yourself? "And He humbled you and let you be hungry." Deut. 8:3. " **Woe** to those who are wise in their own eyes and clever in their own eyes." Is. 5:21. "Do you see a man wise in his own eyes? There is **more hope for a fool** than for him." Prov. 26:12. "For anyone who thinks he is something when he is nothing, **he deceives himself**." Gal. 6:3. "Surely God will not listen to vanity, neither will the Almighty regard it." Job 35:13. "For all of us have become like one who is unclean, and all our righteous deeds are like a **filthy garment**; and all of us wither like a leaf and our iniquities, like the wind take us away." Is. 64:6.

"An arrogant man stirs up strife, but he who trusts in the Lord will prosper. He who trusts in his own heart is a **fool**, but he who walks wisely will be delivered." Prov. 28:25-26. "And he said to them, 'You are those who justify yourselves in the sight of men, but God knows your hearts; for that which is highly esteemed among men is **detestable** in the sight of God.'" Luke 16:15.

Can you see anywhere in Scripture where God instructs us to build up our self-esteem? Or do you find anywhere in Scripture where God instructs us to teach our children to have self-esteem? Are we to pride ourselves in what we have done, or made, or accomplished? What will our flattering do to others, especially our children?

How Do We Begin to Change?

Confess your sins. "Therefore, confess your sins to one another, and pray for one another, so that you may be healed. The effective prayer of a righteous man can accomplish much." James 5:16. Pray for an opportunity to talk to your wife so you can ask for forgiveness for your anger. Don't ramble on and on justifying yourself or blaming her for your anger. Just tell her honestly that God has convicted you of being angry and argumentative. Tell her that with the Lord's help you can change. When you see your children, ask for forgiveness, and explain to them how God is going to help you to change. Each time you blow up, confess to those who have been hurt by your anger. Continue to ask for forgiveness.

Stumbles. This verse separates the men from the boys, or, actually, the righteous from the wicked. Which one will you prove to be? "For a righteous man falls **seven times**, and *rises again*, but the wicked stumble in time of calamity." Prov. 24:16. You will stumble even after you have humbled yourself and confessed your past failures. "Therefore let him who thinks he stands take heed lest he fall." 1Cor. 10:12. The only way to be victorious is to continue to get up again and confess over and over again. Each confession will bring about more humility, and, therefore, more grace will abound. This will lead to victory over this area of sin in your life. "God is opposed to the proud, but gives grace to the humble. Humble yourselves, therefore, under the mighty hand of God, that *He* may exalt you at the proper time." 1Pet. 5:5-6.

First be reconciled. If you don't feel "led" to get things right with your wife and children, don't go back into church. "If therefore you are presenting your offering at the altar, and there remember that your brother has something against you, leave your offering there before the altar, and go your way; **first** be reconciled to your brother, *and then* come and present your offering." Matt. 5:23-24. Be sure you are humble. Are you too proud to admit that you are an angry man? Remember, "God is opposed to the proud, but gives grace to the humble. Humble yourselves, therefore, under the mighty hand of God, that *He* may exalt you at the proper time." 1Pet. 5:5-6.

Personal commitment: To put away my angry ways. "Based on what I have learned from God's Word, I commit to refuse the excusing of my anger or blaming others for it. I commit to daily renewing my mind and being a doer of the Word by putting away my angry ways."

Date: 9/2/17 Signed:

Chapter 7

Thrusts of a Sword

"There is one who speaks rashly like
Thrusts of a sword,
But the tongue of the wise
Brings healing."
Proverbs 12:18

God *spoke* the entire universe into existence. The Lord told us that we would be judged by *every* word we speak. Yet, we often hear it said that we should "speak our mind." When searching the Scriptures, what does God have to say about the tongue? Lets discover the **truth**:

The Tongue, Small yet Deadly

Set on fire by hell. "So also the tongue is a small part of the body, and yet it boasts of great things...And the tongue is a fire, the very world of iniquity; the **tongue** is set among our members as that which **defiles the entire body**, and sets on fire the course of our life, and is set on fire by hell." James 3:5-6.

No one can tame the tongue. "But no one can tame the **tongue**; it is a restless evil and full of deadly poison. With it we bless our Lord and Father; and with it we curse men, who have been made in the likeness of God; from the same mouth come *both blessing and cursing*. My brethren, these things ought not to be this way. Does a fountain send out from the same opening both *fresh and bitter water*?" James 3:8-11. But thank the Lord that "Nothing will be impossible with God." Luke 1:37.

The Lord knows. Here is a sobering thought: "Even before there is a word on my **tongue**, behold O Lord, Thou dost know it all." Ps. 139:4.

We need a muzzle! "I said, 'I will guard my ways, that I may not sin with my **tongue**; I will *guard* my **mouth** as with a muzzle.'" Ps. 39:1. You may have great physical strength, but how about the inner strength required for self-control?

Crushes the spirit. "A *soothing* **tongue** is a tree of life, but perversion in it crushes the spirit." Prov. 15:4. Are the words you speak to your wife, your children, or those at your place of work soothing? Ask yourself if you have been crushing the spirit of those you are to protect and lead.

What We Say

"The mouth of the righteous flows with wisdom, but the **perverted tongue** will be cut out." Prov. 10:31. "There is one who **speaks rashly** like *thrusts of a sword*, but the **tongue of the wise** *brings healing*." Prov. 10:31.

"He who **guards his mouth** and **his tongue** guards his soul from trouble." Prov. 21:23.

This statement is clear. What you say *is* important. "For by **your words** you shall be *justified*, and by **your words** you shall be *condemned*." Matt. 12:37.

"Not what enters into the mouth that defiles the man, but what **proceeds out of the mouth**, this defiles the man." Matt. 15:11.

"...put them all aside; anger, wrath, malice, **slander** and **abusive speech**...." Col.3:8. "He who gives **attention to the word** shall find good." Prov. 16:20.

If you have abused your wife with your words, God is faithful; He offers a cure:

"**Pleasant words** are a honeycomb, sweet to the soul and healing to the bones." Prov. 16:24. "**Sweetness of speech** increases persuasiveness." Prov. 16:20.

"**Righteous lips** are the delight of kings, and he who **speaks right** is loved." Prov. 16:13.

Have you matured? Perhaps you remember this childhood phrase, "Sticks and stones may break my bones, but words will never hurt me." The fact is many of us probably still haven't recovered from some of the harsh words that were spoken to us as children. Do you continue to hurt your wife or your children with your words? "When I was a child, I used to **speak as a child**, think as a child, reason as a child; when I became a man, **I did away with childish things**." 1Cor. 13:11.

How We Answer

A gentle answer. When anger or wrath is directed toward us, God tells us the response we must make as Christians in order to glorify Him. "A **gentle answer** turns away wrath, but harsh words stir up anger." Prov. 15:1.

Ponders how to answer. Do you think before you speak? "The heart of the righteous **ponders how to answer** but the mouth of the wicked pours out evil things." Prov. 15:28. Do you *pour out* evil words on other people?

Folly and shame. Do you halfway listen or cut off the other person before they've had a chance to share their thought with you or ask a question? "He who gives an **answer before he hears**, it is folly and shame to him." Prov. 18:13. Give your wife an opportunity to get everything off her chest. Ask her questions so you are sure you understand what she is trying to tell you and why. Is she in need of empathy? Give her a listening and understanding ear. Or, perhaps, she needs help discerning something that just "talking it out" will accomplish.

Many times your wife doesn't want you to fix her problems. She needs and wants understanding and encouragement. This sometimes takes a lot of patience, but patience is the proof of your love. "Love is patient..." 1Cor. 13:4. Are you doing all you can to be patient with your wife? Prove your love for her by being patient and understanding. "You husbands likewise, live with your wives in an understanding way...." 1Pet. 3:7.

Washed with the Word. Do you bless your wife with God's Word and with *your* loving, edifying words? "Husbands, love your wives, just as Christ also loved the church and gave Himself up for her; that He might sanctify her, having cleansed her by the *washing* of water **with the word** that He might present to Himself the church in all her glory, having no spot or wrinkle or any such thing; but that she should be holy and blameless." Eph. 5:25.

How *Much* You Say

Many words. When there is a lot of talking and discussing, transgression (a violation of God's Law) cannot be avoided. "With **many words transgression is unavoidable.**" Prov. 10:19. As the leader, direct lengthy discussions properly to a conclusion. This does not mean that you are to cut your wife off when it's her turn to share her thoughts, or drop a hurtful "bomb" and then say the matter is finished. Be sure you have understood her. Make sure she knows you understand by giving her a positive and loving response. Most women keep on talking because they don't feel they are being understood.

Guards his mouth. Are you careful to guard what you say to others, especially your wife? There are those who tell us to speak our mind and to share what we think, but God says, "A *man of understanding* keeps **silent**." Prov. 11:12. And, "One who **guards** his mouth preserves his life; one who opens it comes to ruin." Prov. 13:3.

Considered wise. Actually, God says that we practice wisdom and appear to be wise when we say nothing. "Even a fool, when he

keeps silent, is *considered wise*. When he **closes his lips** he is counted as prudent." Prov. 17:28.

Anything more. "But let your statement be, **'Yes, yes' or 'No, no'** - anything beyond these is of evil." Matt. 5:37. Nod your head up and down when your wife is talking to you. If you keep your eyes and mind on what she is trying to tell you, rather than watching the television, reading the paper, or thinking of something else, your conversation will satisfy your wife's need to be heard and understood much more quickly.

Empty chatter. "Guard what has been entrusted to you, **avoiding worldly and empty chatter** and the opposing arguments of what is falsely called 'knowledge' - which some have professed and thus gone astray from the faith." 1Tim 6:20. When you must make a decision, you do not need to argue *your* point of view. Just state your decision based on prayer and God's leading. When your wife sees that your heart is striving to follow the right way, the Lord's way, and that you are not using your authority to get your own way, then she will stop trying to control or manipulate you.

Be Content, Stop Grumbling

Do all things... "Do all things without **grumbling or disputing.**" Phil. 2:14. Do you sometimes find yourself grumbling about a task before you do it? Now, if it's something you know you should be doing, do it and don't grumble or dispute it! Yet, if you are being "railroaded" into doing something you don't think you should, don't do it. Remember the trouble it got Adam (and all of us) into. "Then to Adam He said, 'Because you have listened to the voice of your wife, and have eaten from the tree about which I commanded **you'**...." Gen. 3:17. "Therefore, to one who knows the right thing to do, and does not do it, to *him* it is sin." James 4:17.

Whatever the circumstances. Are you someone who has to complain about everything that happens to you? You must learn contentment. "Not that I speak from want; for I have *learned* to be **content** in whatever circumstances I am." Phil. 4:11. Are you setting a good example for your wife and children? Are you, as the head of your household, demonstrating to your family how to be content or are you teaching them to grumble and complain?

Great gain. Godliness and contentment must go hand in hand. "But **godliness** is actually a means of great gain, when accompanied by **contentment**." 1Tim. 6:6.

Are you content? "...being **content** with what you have; for He Himself has said, 'I will never desert you, nor will I ever forsake you.' " Heb. 13:5. Are you satisfied with what you have, or are you constantly trying to upgrade all your "toys" and possessions?

Crushes the spirit. Proverbs also tells us what our speech can do to our wife's spirit. "A **soothing tongue** is a **tree of life**, but **perversion** (defined as "obstinate") in it **crushes the spirit**." Prov. 15:4. Is your wife less affectionate to you then she used to be? Maybe, without realizing it, you have crushed her spirit.

Is Arguing *Good* For Marriage?

A dry morsel. Some "experts" say that arguing can actually be good for a marriage. What does God say? "Better is a dry morsel and quietness with it, than a house full of feasting with strife." Prov. 17:1. Strife is defined as a prolonged struggle for power or superiority. There should be no struggle for power or superiority if each one in the family knows their role and each one concentrates on fulfilling that role. Strife comes when these duties are neglected or when each person is too busy seeing to it that the *other* person is doing what they should.

On the subject of quietness, be sure your children are quiet and under *your* control! It's not only your wife's responsibility to keep them quiet. Your presence should warrant respect and silence. (See Lesson 14 "Father's Instructions" in the Men's Manual.)

Abandon the quarrel. Do you abandon the quarrel, or do you fight until you win? "The beginning of strife is like letting out water, so **abandon** the **quarrel** before it breaks out." Prov. 17:14. Again, you do not need to struggle, argue, or prove yourself to be the head of your home. God has given you the leadership position. However, this should **never** be a place of pride or arrogance. Your headship is to be used to guide, protect and manage your family wisely under God's direction.

Any fool will quarrel. "A fool's lips bring strife, and his mouth calls for blows." Prov. 18:6. Perhaps your wife may even take a swing at you if your words are extremely painful to her. Of course, she is no match for you so this could then enter into an abusive situation. Remember to **abandon** the **quarrel** before it breaks out! She would be wrong for throwing a punch or for possibly starting the verbal fighting, but you are to be the leader and savior of the body. "For the husband is the **head** of the wife, as Christ also is the head of the church, He Himself being the **Savior** of the body." Eph. 5:23. Remember, "... **any fool will quarrel!**" Prov. 20:3.

Dealt treacherously. "...the LORD has been a witness between you and the wife of your youth, against whom you have **dealt treacherously**, though she is your companion and your wife by covenant. But **not one** has done so who has a **remnant** of the **Spirit**. And what did that one do while he was seeking a godly offspring? Take heed then, to your spirit, and let no one deal treacherously against the wife of your youth." Mal. 2:14-15.

If you have dealt treacherously with your wife, then God is saying to you that you have not even a remnant of His Spirit! That is a sobering thought! Let's each take a hard look at ourselves and get right with God, then our relationship with our wives will follow.

Covers his garment with wrong. " 'For I hate divorce,' says the LORD, the God of Israel, and him who covers his garment with wrong,' says the LORD of hosts. 'So take heed to your spirit, that you do not deal treacherously.'" Mal. 2:16. Treacherously in the Hebrew translation is defined as to deal deceitfully, unfaithfully, offend, transgress, or depart.

To cover your garment with wrong is defined as violence, unjust gain, cruel, injustice or an oppressor. Many men are in a physical battle or emotional battle with their wives. We have all seen or known women who try to act as tough as men, but are they? Can they ever be? Think about sports that require physical strength, can men and women ever compete fairly? Have you ever witnessed a situation where a successful businesswoman gave way to tears? From her outward appearance, you may have been fooled into thinking that she was every bit as emotionally tough as a man.

It is the hope of this ministry that your wife, after seeing a change in you, will desire to read the Workbook for Women. This will encourage her to seek a gentle and quiet spirit; allowing herself to be the weaker vessel. But how will you respond to her? Will you crush her or cherish her? (Prov. 15:4, Eph. 5:29.)

Agree, Especially With Your Wife

Agree. One of the most important principles taught in the New Testament concerns agreeing with someone, especially when the other person is angry. "**Agree** with thine **adversary** quickly, while thou art in the way with him...." Matt. 5:25 KJV. Listening and nodding your head will help a lot when someone is angry or frustrated. So many times we play the "devil's advocate" trying to show someone the other side. (The name alone should warn us of the probable consequences!) Give your wife a chance to share her thoughts, feelings, and frustrations. Get on her side - and don't fuel the fire.

Divided against itself. Satan will do all he can to illuminate the areas where you *don't agree* so he can divide and conquer your family. "Any kingdom divided against itself is laid waste; and any city or house divided against itself shall not stand." Matt. 12:25. And, "Any kingdom divided against itself is laid waste; and a house divided against itself falls." Luke 11:17. "Keeping away from strife is an honor for a man, but **any fool will quarrel**." Prov. 20:3.

Agreement. This verse shows us why satan works so hard to cause disagreement between Christian couples. "Again I say to you, that if two of you agree on earth about anything that they may ask, it shall be done for them by My Father who is in heaven." Matt. 18:19.

When we don't agree as a couple, we actually cancel each other out. It's just as if you were going to vote for opposing political candidates, you might as well stay home. "But **refuse foolish and ignorant speculations** knowing that **they produce quarrels**. And the Lord's bond- servant must not be quarrelsome, but be kind to all, able to teach, patient when wronged." 2Tim. 2:23.

Deeds of the flesh are evident. It is evident to other Christians, and certainly to God, when the way we act is of a fleshly nature. "Deeds of the flesh are evident...**strife**, jealousy, **outbursts of anger, disputes, dissensions**, envying...." Gal. 5:19-21. "If any one advocates a different doctrine and **does not agree with sound words**, those of our Lord Jesus Christ, and with the doctrine conforming to godliness, he is conceited and understands nothing; but he has a morbid interest in controversial questions and **disputes** about words, out of which arise envy, **strife, abusive language**, evil suspicions, and **constant friction** between men of **depraved mind** and **deprived of the truth**...." 1Tim. 6:3-5.

Fruit of the Spirit. "But the fruit of the Spirit is **love, joy, peace, patience, kindness, goodness, faithfulness, gentleness, self-control**; against such things there is no law." Gal. 5:22. "Urge bondslaves to be subject to their own masters in everything, to be well-pleasing, not argumentative." Titus 2:9. As a Christian, you are the Lord's bondslave. He bought you with a price. You are not your wife's bondslave. You, as Christ's bondslave, need to be pleasing to *Him*.

Anger of man. You have heard some say that since Jesus was angry and turned over the tables in the temple, we can be angry. "But let everyone be **quick to hear; slow to speak** and **slow to anger**; for the **anger of man does not achieve the righteousness of God**." James 1:19-20.

Again, agree! You must try to find the area of agreement instead of the point of disagreement. "Again I say that if two of you **agree** on earth about anything that they may ask, it shall be done for them by My Father who is in heaven." Matt. 18:19. Take charge of a disagreement. Nod your head, find the points you agree on, and state them to her out loud. Wives want to be heard, everyone does.

That's why people get louder and begin screaming or yelling – they want to be heard and understood. Take time to consider the areas where you agree and move in that direction.

A Lying Tongue

The Lord hates. Let's read Proverbs, which tells us much about lying. "There are six things which the Lord hates, Yes, seven which are an abomination to Him: Haughty eyes, a **lying tongue** and hands that shed innocent blood..." Prov. 6:16-18.

Deceitful. "Deliver my soul, O Lord from **lying** lips, from a **deceitful** tongue." Ps. 120:2. When your wife, or someone else, catches you in a lie (or what you may call a fib), do you deny it? Are you truthful? Or do you debate about exactly what you said to try and twist the truth to your favor? Remember, deceitful is in the definition of dealing treacherously with your wife.

Father of lies. Be sure that you **never lie**, because **the devil is the father of lies**, and lying is an abomination to God. "You are of your father the devil, and you want to do the desires of your father. He was a murderer from the beginning, and does not stand in the truth, because there is no truth in him. Whenever he speaks a **lie**, he speaks from his own nature; for he is a **liar**, and the **father of lies**." John 8:44. Remember, it's the truth that sets you free!

Impossible To Control When Drinking

Not wise. "Wine is a mocker, strong drink a brawler, And whoever is intoxicated by it is not wise." Prov. 20:1. The person who is intoxicated by the effects of alcohol is not wise. What you speak while intoxicated will mock you later. "And you neglected all my counsel, And did not want my reproof; I will even laugh at your calamity; I will mock when your dread comes...." Prov. 1:25-26. "And do not get drunk with wine, for that is dissipation (frivolous amusement), but be filled with the Spirit...." Eph. 5:18.

Utter perverse things. "Who has woe? Who has sorrow? Who has **contentions**? Who has complaining? Who has wounds without cause? Who has redness of eyes? Those who linger long over wine, those who go to taste mixed wine. Do not look on the wine when it is red, when it sparkles in the cup, when it goes down smoothly; at the last it bites like a serpent, and stings like a viper. Your eyes will see strange things, and your mind will **utter perverse things**. And you will be like one who lies down in the middle of the sea, or like one who lies down on the top of a mast. 'They struck me, but I did not become ill; they beat me, but I did not know it. When shall I awake? I will seek another drink.' " Prov. 23:29-35.

A person who drinks a lot is not an alcoholic. Drinking to excess is not a disease; it's a sin. Confess your sin if you are held by the cords of alcohol. If you stumble, continue to confess and cry out to God for deliverance.

Proceeds out. "Not what enters into the mouth defiles the man, but what proceeds **out of the mouth**, this defiles the man." Matt. 15:11. If what you are putting into yourself causes your lips to transgress, then you should stop. Do it for your wife, your children, or others who are close to you. Confess your sin and move on to victory! "...the truth shall make you free." John 8:32. Hallelujah!

To Sum Up...

1. Be aware of **how much** you say: With **many words** transgression is unavoidable. Instead, let your communication be **Yes, yes** or **No, no** - anything more than this will lead to evil.

2. Be **careful** *what* you say: by **your words** you'll be justified and by **your words** you'll be condemned!

3. Do not argue: **agree** with your **adversary** *quickly*!

4. How are we to answer? Give a gentle answer, ponder (think a while) how to answer, and don't answer before you listen,

it is folly and shame!

5. Learn to **be content** in whatever circumstances you are in.

6. If healing is needed: remember, **pleasant words** are a honeycomb, sweet to the soul and healing to the bones, and **sweetness** of speech **adds persuasiveness.**

7. You must **walk in the Spirit** and stop doing whatever you please. "But I say, walk by the Spirit, and you will not carry out the desire of the flesh...these are in opposition to one another, so that you **may not** do the things that you please."

8. The rule of thumb that will help to guide you is this: whatever comes easy for us to do in the flesh is of the flesh. Whatever is difficult to do and requires us to draw on the Holy Spirit's strength is walking in the Spirit.

Strive to appear wise by keeping silent.

Let your words be loving and patient.

Love your wife as Christ loves His church.

Personal Commitment: To open my mouth with wisdom and healing. "Based on what I have learned from God's Word, I commit to remain patient, wait before I answer, and to be sweet in my every word, especially to my wife and children."

Date: _____ Signed: _____

May God be with you as you strive to be more like Christ!

Chapter 8

Have You Dealt Treacherously?

*"The LORD has been a witness between
You and the wife of your youth, against
Whom you have dealt treacherously,
Though she is your companion
And your wife by covenant."*
Malachi 2:14

Have you dealt treacherously with your wife?

Maybe that question is difficult to answer because you're not exactly sure what the Bible means by living treacherously. If we check the Strong's Concordance, the word treacherous, "bagad" pronounced (*baw-gad*), means **to act covertly, to pillage, deal deceitfully, offend, transgress, depart, unfaithful.**

The definition of *treacherous* in the Webster's dictionary is: of the character or actions of a traitor.

Now that you have the definition, you must ask yourself; have you committed any of these offenses against your wife? Let's take each offense and look at it carefully. This is not intended to condemn you, but rather to bring you to conviction. Until there is conviction and you look at your actions as sin, there can be no repentance. And without repentance, there is no mercy. Without mercy, there is no grace. And, brother, we all need as much grace as we can get! We can deny our sins all we want, but that will never bring about the change that is needed. You need to be the kind of husband your wife needs (and deserves)! If you're ready, then let's go.

To act covertly. The definition of *covert* is hidden, secret or disguised. How many times have you hidden things or done things secretly? "But all things become visible when they are exposed by the light, for everything that becomes visible is light." Eph. 5:13. You may have covered it up with everyone, even your wife, but there *is* One from whom you cannot hide. If you have done things in secret, then you have dealt treacherously with your wife.

To pillage is the act of taking goods by force, also to attack, defraud, or rob. You may be looking at this in the context of actual material goods, but what is most important to a woman is not the material goods, but the *emotional* goods. Have you attacked her verbally, or have you robbed her of joy because of your anger? Have you also robbed her of joy because of the unrealistic demands that you have put on her? Have you been a man that continually takes from her, giving very little in return? Now do you wonder why your marriage is in the state that it is in? My friend, there is a Savior who is waiting for you to lay this all down at the cross. HE is there to forgive you, if you repent.

Dealing deceitfully. Most of us are so good at talking around the truth, and our excuse is that we can't tell our wives the truth because we don't want to hurt them. Or, when we *are* confronted with the truth, we tell our wife that it's her fault because, *you always get on me and I don't need a mother.* Well, do we need a mother? If there is nothing wrong with what we are doing, why do we need to hide it?

Let's take a hard look at Scripture and stop making excuses. "A false witness will not go unpunished, and **he who tells lies will not escape.**" Prov. 19:5. Also, as we learned in the last chapter, "There are six things which the LORD hates, Yes, seven which are an **abomination** to Him: Haughty eyes, a **lying tongue**, and hands that shed innocent blood, a heart that devises wicked plans, feet that run rapidly to evil, a false witness who **utters lies**, and one who spreads strife among brothers." Prov. 6:16-19.

Offend. When you offend your wife, do you really care? Or do you just think or say *it's her problem*. Men and women were created and brought together to complement one another. Our wives need our strength and leadership, and we men most desperately need our wife's refinement.

How do you dress? What about those comfortable clothes you wear around the house that she finds so unappealing? What you wear in the presence of your wife speaks volumes as to how much or how little you care. How are your manners? Do you open doors for her and help her put her coat on? Do you treat your wife with honor? What are you teaching your children by your poor example?

Transgress. Webster says that to transgress means to go beyond a limit. Men and women both have a limit to how much they can take before they actually break. It may be that they break physically or emotionally. One of three things usually happens when a person is pushed beyond what they can endure: they learn to fight back, they walk away, or they stay until they are destroyed. Whose fault is it if you push your own wife too far? "And He said to His disciples, 'It is inevitable that stumbling blocks should come, but woe to him **through whom** they come!' " Luke 17:1.

Depart. It is sad to see so many men leaving their families only to find new wives and new families for which to care. It is so frustrating to see these men paying so much attention to children that are not their own, while at the same time their own children are falling apart emotionally due to their abandonment. "Like a bird that wanders from her nest, So is a man who wanders from his home." Prov. 27:8.

Unfaithful. Have you ever been unfaithful to your wife? Many of us have to hang our heads in shame and say "yes." But for those of you who think that you got off on this one, let's look deeper. In our world today, this godless, sinful, perverted society, to be unfaithful is nothing short of laying with a woman that is not your wife. However, unfaithful *also* means: failing one's trust; disloyal. Have you ever failed when your wife trusted in you? Have you ever put your loyalty to someone else above your loyalty to your wife? You know that you are to be "one" with the woman God has joined you with. This other person to whom you were loyal does not have to be someone of the opposite sex; they could be a friend or a family member.

One of the most damaging and conflicting ties can be with your mother or your father. How do we know? Because the Lord Himself made special reference to it: "But from the beginning of creation, God made them male and female. For this cause a man shall leave his father and mother, and the two shall become one flesh; consequently they are no longer two, but one flesh." Mark 10:6.

Abuse

Abuse my wife? You may deny that you abuse her because you never laid a hand on her. Or you may say you're not an abusive husband because you didn't throw the first punch. Lets find out what abuse really is.

In the Webster's dictionary, *abuse* is defined as: to misuse, to ill-treat, injure, to call someone foul names. Foul is defined as: to bring dishonor, indecent or profane, obnoxious or unpleasant.

Misuse. God has blessed us with a wife. "He who finds a wife finds a good thing, and obtains favor from the LORD." Prov. 18:22. And "Then the LORD God said, 'It is not good for the man to be alone....'" Gen. 2:18.

God certainly had a good reason to bless you with a wife; however, she was not for you to use improperly or incorrectly. Your wife is (or was) a gift from God. Have you treated her that way?

Injure. Also in Webster's, *injure* is defined as to inflict a wound or other physical hurt upon, to cause intangible or other physical hurt: to injure someone's feelings. The Psalmist said, "Let those who are adversaries of my soul be ashamed and consumed; let them be covered with reproach and dishonor, who seek to **injure** me." Ps. 71:13. God knows what is done in secret. "For nothing is hidden that shall not become evident, nor anything secret that shall not be known and come to light." Luke 8:17. Let us not forget what the title verse is, "...**the LORD has been a witness** between you and the wife of your youth, against whom you have dealt treacherously, though she is your companion and your wife by covenant." Mal. 2:14.

To call someone foul names. Again, *foul* is defined as: to bring dishonor, indecent or profane, obnoxious or unpleasant. We just read in the previous chapter "Thrusts of a Sword" about the tongue and the horrible results, which come when a person cannot control the contents of what they say. Unfortunately, many of us would never want to admit that when we say things to our wives that are unpleasant that we are abusing (misusing) what God has given to us. "You husbands likewise, live with your wives in an understanding way, as with a weaker vessel, since she is a woman; and grant her honor as a fellow heir of the grace of life, so that your prayers may not be hindered." 1Pet. 3:7.

The Violent Man

Does the Bible even mention the violent man?

Yes. Many Scriptures, especially the Psalms, give us insight into the violent man. As a matter of fact, the entire 140th Psalm is about the violent man... "Rescue me, O Lord from evil men; preserve me from **violent men**, who devise evil things in their hearts; they continually stir up wars. They sharpen their tongues as a serpent; poison of a viper is under their lips. Keep me O Lord, from the hands of the wicked; preserve me from **violent men** who have purposed to trip up my feet." Ps. 140:1-4. Is this a description of you? Be honest with yourself. Have you ever devised an evil plan against your wife, a way to get even, or teach her a lesson? Do you stir up wars or arguments? Does she ask you to stop speaking cruel words to her? Do you ignore her cries? Do you twist her words and what she is saying for the purpose of tripping her up? If so, then *you* are a violent man.

The violent man. "The Lord lives and blessed be my rock; and exalted be God the rock of my salvation, the God who executes vengeance for me, and brings down peoples under me, who also brings me out from my enemies; Thou dost even lift me above those who rise up against me; Thou dost rescue me from **the violent man**." 2Sam. 22:47-49. The wife who trusts the Lord will see herself rescued from a violent husband. Perhaps this has already happened. Is this why she has left you or asked you to leave? Maybe you are still denying that you are a violent man. Let us look more deeply into the Word of God for more truth.

What does the word "violent" really mean?

Cruel. The word violent in the Greek language is *chamac* which means to maltreat, make bare, violate, to be **cruel,** or to cause a false injustice. Be honest with yourself. Does this describe you?

The Lord has been a witness. "Because **the Lord has been a witness** between you and the wife of your youth, against whom you have dealt treacherously, though she is your wife by covenant. But not one has done so who has a remnant of the Spirit…Take heed then, to your spirit, and let no one deal treacherously against the wife of your youth. 'For I hate divorce', says the Lord, the God of Israel, 'and him who covers his garment with wrong,' says the Lord of hosts. So take heed to your spirit, that you do not deal treacherously." Mal. 2:14-16.

Root Causes of Abuse and Misuse Why do I treat my wife this way?

When we violate Biblical principles, we suffer the consequences. There are guidelines for the married man, and violating these guidelines will lay a foundation for insensitivity to the "wife of your youth."

Cleave to wife. "For this cause a man shall leave his father and his mother, and shall cleave to his wife; and they shall become one flesh." Gen. 2:24. Cleaving is defined as "a desperate holding onto." This is quite clearly not happening today since so many of us leave our wives.

Are you still trying to please or get approval from the family that you should have left? We are to honor our parents, but, clearly, Scripture says that we are also to honor our wife. "You husbands likewise, live with your wives in an understanding way, as with a weaker vessel, since she is a woman; and grant her honor as a fellow heir of the grace of life, so that your prayers may not be hindered." 1Pet. 3:7.

When you have a division between what your wife may think or feel and what your parents think or feel, what is a man to do? Whom should he honor? Jesus told us by quoting Genesis, "For this cause a man shall leave his father and mother, and shall cleave to his wife; and the two shall become one flesh." Matt. 19:5. He also said, "Consequently they are no longer two, but one flesh. What therefore God has joined together, let no man separate." Matt. 19:6.

Still tied. Take a moment to ponder this; perhaps you have not really "left" your mother and/or father. Sure you have left physically, but are you still tied to them since your loyalty has remained with your parents? Leave your parents, cleave to your wife, and rejoice in the wife of your youth! (Prov. 5:18.)

Love. "Husbands, love your wives, just as Christ also loved...." Eph. 5:25. "So husbands ought also to love their own wives...." Eph. 5:28. "Husbands, love your wives, and do not be embittered against them." Col. 3:19. Ever since the feminist movement permeated the church with lies, there has been a "blending" of the roles and commandments given to men and women. We continue to hear others say that God commanded men and women to love their spouses. This "command" was only given to the husband. Actually, the only "reference" for a woman to love her husband is given in Titus, where the older woman is encouraged to *teach* the younger to love her husband and her children. "You shall not add to the word which I am commanding you...." Deut. 4:2. Does that mean a wife isn't to love her husband? Emphatically no! "...and walk in love, just as Christ also loved you, and gave Himself up for us...." Eph. 5:2.

Since our wife is asked to respect and submit to us, we should make it easy for her by loving her as we are commanded to in Ephesians 5. Does your wife have trouble respecting you? Pray for opportunities to gain her respect. Do something that would require character, humility or some other attribute that may be lacking in you.

In short, show her a godly man. The result will be a deep love for you. "We love, because He first loved us." 1John 4:19. Our wives will love us because of our love for God. When we follow His commands, we will become more like Him.

Separate us? A husband who shows true love for his wife, the way he is commanded, will be protected from separation or divorce. "Who shall separate us from the love of Christ? Shall tribulation, or distress, or persecution, or famine, or nakedness, or peril, or sword?" Rom. 8:35.

Love controls us. Your love for your wife will motivate her to do as you ask, just as love is our children's motivation to obey us as their parents. "For the love of Christ controls us...." 2Cor. 5:14.

Walk in love. Saying you love her is not enough. Sometimes our actions speak louder than our words. "...and walk in love, just as Christ also loved you, and gave Himself up for us...." Eph. 5:2. If you live separately from your wife, begin now to treat her the way you should. Show her the love that is described in 1Cornthians chapter 13, which is unconditional, non-judgmental whenever you have an opportunity to see, write or talk to her.

One flesh. "So the LORD God caused a deep sleep to fall upon the man, and he slept; then He took one of his ribs, and closed up the flesh at that place. And the LORD God fashioned into a woman the rib which He had taken from the man, and brought her to the man. And the man said, 'This is now bone of my bones, and flesh of my flesh; she shall be called woman, because she was taken out of man.' " Gen. 2:21. "AND THE TWO SHALL BECOME ONE

FLESH; consequently they are no longer two, but one flesh." Mark 10:8. "Consequently they are no longer two, but one flesh. What therefore God has joined together, let no man separate." Matt. 19:6.

A woman doesn't desire physical oneness as much as she desires her husband to be "one" with her emotionally, spiritually, and mentally. Do you and your wife have the same goals and directions? Did you allow or encourage division in your home? Did you encourage your wife to pursue a degree or career that has eventually caused division? God created woman to help and complete the man. Once a marriage takes place, they are "no longer two, but one flesh." This means that they live their lives together in one accord. They are not to live as "roommates" with each having their own life apart from the other.

Man independent of woman? We are to be one flesh in our heart and our desires. God created women with certain needs, and we, as men, also have needs. The voids in my life and in my wife's life were created as a type of working gear that fits together perfectly as we meet each other's needs.

When we fill our voids ourselves or apart from our wife, the gear slips. The more we fill or the more our wife fills her voids inappropriately, the more our relationship slips until there is nothing left to hang on to. The world tells our wives to fulfill *their* needs and to let us as men fend for ourselves. Co-dependency is a popular psychological fad these days to convince us that it is not good for a husband and wife to be dependent upon each other. But what does God's Word say about our dependency for one another as a married couple?

"However, in the Lord, neither is woman independent of man, nor is man independent of woman. For as the woman originates from the man." 1Cor. 11:11-12. When we violate God's ways, we reap the consequences. Pray for opportunities to meet your wife's needs right now, even if you are not in the home.

In toil. "Then to Adam He said, 'Because you have listened to the voice of your wife, and have eaten from the tree about which I commanded you, saying, 'You shall not eat from it'; Cursed is the ground because of you; In toil you shall eat of it all the days of your life." Gen. 3:17. After the fall of man, the man and the woman were each given a punishment. The woman was given pain in childbirth, and the man was to toil the ground or work. So why is the man's punishment now shared by both the man and the woman?

When women earn their own money apart from their husband's, they can make their own decisions about how it is to be spent. When wives have a different career than that of the home and children, it divides the couple's interests and makes them independent from each other. This is exactly what happens when wives work outside the home as a second provider.

Protector. When your wife protects herself because she feels she can (or has to) "fight her own battles," why does she need you? Is it your wife who tells that salesperson off or gets rid of "that guy at the door?" Have you forgotten how to handle these situations? Who really wears the pants in the family; who really is stronger?

We must acknowledge that many times our wives have taken over because of our neglect. Either we didn't take on the challenge, or we were absent because of our job, hobby or whatever. Once you can acknowledge this, you will be able to confess your shortcomings as a protector to your wife. You must then begin to take on each challenge that comes against your family. You might say that you would attack anyone trying to kill a member of your family, but what about the bad waiter at the restaurant, the rude repairman? What about your disrespectful teenager? Do you allow attacks on your wife? Are your children keenly aware that they would have *you* to contend with if they even looked the wrong way at their mother? Even if you are living apart, pray for an opportunity to show her your ability to protect her.

Ask their own husbands at home. Men, are you the leader in spiritual matters? Does your wife run to ask you what you think as the spiritual leader, or would she say, "Why would I go to him?" "What does he know, I'm the one going to all the Bible studies, seminars, and even sitting on all the church committees!" Her desire is for you to be the spiritual leader. "Her husband is known in the gates, when he sits among the elders of the land." Prov. 31:23.

But many of us seem to have more important things to do than to lead our family spiritually, like playing a sport, working at hobbies, hunting, watching television or a movie, or just meeting the "guys." After all, if your wife or children have a spiritual question, they have the pastor or the Sunday school teacher to go to for answers. "And if they desire to learn anything, let them ask their own husbands at home; for it is improper for a woman to speak in church." 1Cor. 14:35. Take the time now to get into God's Word and prepare yourself.

Father. Husbands clearly have been pushed out of their role as fathers. Many men are criticized for the way they handle, or treat, the children so often that they just stop "interfering." God gave each of us a mother and a father with their distinct characteristics so we could grow up without a bunch of hang-ups or emotional troubles. Children need both parents. But, again, if the roles are blended and blurred, who needs a father? "Honor your father and mother; and you shall love your neighbor as yourself." Matt. 19:19. When you have your children with you, keep them in line and teach them to obey and show respect to their mother when they are with her. (This goes for children of any age: 5, 15, or 25!)

Who should be the Spiritual Leader?

One question many women ask is: "Who should be the Spiritual Leader since my husband won't or doesn't do it?" Or, many women will state, "I *have* to be the Spiritual leader of our home because my husband is not even a Christian!" Why are so many men neglecting or forfeiting their position as the spiritual head of their family?

Her husband is known. All Christian women desire their husband to be the spiritual leader. "**Her husband is known** in the gates, when he sits among the elders of the land." Prov. 31: 23. Women many times have had to take over the leadership positions. The world's philosophy has destroyed our nation, and it is destroying the church. Men have neglected their positions in the church. They have left to pursue other interests. When men left the church, many of the wives fell into the hands of liberated pastors that have taken many women captive. "For among them are those who enter into households and captivate weak women weighed down with sins, led on by various impulses, always learning and never able to come to the knowledge of the truth." 2Tim. 3:6-7.

Good for nothing. Too many churches are now overrun, for the most part, with weak men and strong women. This is causing ineffectiveness in the church because many of the men are MIA! "You are the salt of the earth; but if the salt has become tasteless, how will it be made salty again? It is good for nothing anymore, except to be thrown out and trampled under foot by men." Matt. 5:13. Get totally involved in church if you have lost your family. Do it now while you have the time.

Be subject to your own husbands in everything. Men have you looked to your wife to lead your family? "Wives be subject to your own husbands, as to the Lord...to their husbands in everything." Eph. 5:22-24. It is clear from the above Scripture that God has put **all** husbands in the Spiritual leadership role of the home. Let's see what happens when things get out of order.

No one can serve two masters. When men neglect to lead their families and to take responsibility for what goes on in their homes, their wife and children will begin to hate them. Remember, you have turned over most of your responsibility to other people or institutions. Why would they listen to you? "No one can serve two masters; for either he will **hate the one** and **love the other**, or he **will hold to one** and **despise the other**." Matt. 6:24.

You often see this when a child who once listened to his parents is sent off to school. All of a sudden, they tell their parents what their teacher said is right and they are now wrong. Some men send their sons and daughters off to college, along with their money (as the bumper sticker says), when those kids return home for break, they treat their fathers like the town idiot! (See Chapter 14 "Father's Instruction" in *A Wise Man*.)

He will do it. Does your wife act as though she is your personal Holy Spirit? Why does she do this? Again, because of your neglect and your stupidity on Spiritual matters. Does your wife know her Bible better than you do? Or worse, are your children better versed in Scripture than you are? Do you as the father make sure that your children are in Sunday school or pay for Christian school, but neglected to know the stuff yourself?

If you think it is too late or that you are too far behind to get ahead of your wife and children to properly lead them, you are wrong. Since God has called you to be the leader of your home, He will enable you to do so.

We must confess our sin of neglect. "Therefore, confess your sins to one another, and pray for one another, so that you may be healed. The effective prayer of a righteous man can accomplish much." James 5:16. Confess to your wife and children. Then pray for opportunities to lead them spiritually. Talk to your children about the Lord and tell them how He's helping you.

Boast about our weaknesses. "And He has said to me, 'My grace is sufficient for you, for power is perfected in weakness.' Most gladly, therefore, I will rather boast about my weaknesses, that the power of Christ may dwell in me." 2Cor. 12:9. When your wife attacks you and points out your failures – jump in, agree with her and boast. This is humility in action!

And above all, trust the Lord. "Commit your way to the lord, trust also in Him, and **He will do it**." Ps. 37:5. If you want to begin leading your family spiritually, begin first with a time of prayer. Then begin reading your Bible regularly. God will lead you and direct your paths if your efforts are sincere.

Washing of water with the Word. Men, you must be extremely careful about what you say to your wife, what you read to your wife, and what you encourage her to look at. "Husbands, love your wives, just as Christ also loved the church and gave Himself up for her; that He might **sanctify her**, having **cleansed her** by the **washing of water with the Word**, that He might present to Himself the church in all her glory, having no spot or wrinkle or any such thing; but that she should be holy and blameless." Eph. 5:25-27.

If you are separated or divorced, read your verses out loud. Then ask the Lord to wash her where she is. Continue after you are together. This is what Hosea did with Gomer: "Therefore, behold, I will allure her, bring her into the wilderness, and speak kindly to her...For I will remove the names of the Baals from her mouth, so that they will be mentioned by their names no more." Hosea 2:14, 17.

You may complain about her nagging or lying or the way she gets into crazy conflicts with you; yet, do you ever stop to think what you are watching as a family every day on television? Is it the stupid sitcom programs where the men are portrayed as buffoons and the women are all contentious comedians? What movies do you saturate your wife and children in? What type of movies are **you** watching? The next time you, your wife, or your family sits down to watch *anything*, just think of it as a "training film." The behavior you and your family are watching will be learned and acted out!

The narrow gate. Men, go through the **narrow gate** and stop spending so much time watching the television. Stop sending your weekly or monthly dues to Hollywood, via the movie theater or video store. "Enter by the **narrow gate**; for the gate is wide, and the way is broad that leads to destruction, and *many are those who enter by it.*" Matt. 7:13.

Stop making lame excuses to cover up your compromising leadership. Spend your time delighting yourself in the Lord. Remember, He promises to give you the desires of your heart. (Ps. 37:4.)

Practicing your righteousness before men. Do you go to church just to let others see the man that you are pretending to be? "Beware of **practicing your righteousness before men** to be noticed by them; otherwise you have **no reward** with your Father who is in heaven." Matt. 6:1. Our actions must be an outpouring of what is in us.

You will know them by their fruits. What are your fruits as a Christian? **"You will know them by their fruits**." Matt. 7:16. If you, as the husband and father, are not leading your family daily in the Word, then you are producing thorns, not fruit. Do you read your Bible daily? If so, for how long? Compare the time you spend reading the newspaper or the sports page versus reading the Word. Are you able to comprehend anything that you are reading in this book? Can anyone see any change in you as a result of reading this book?

"For if anyone is a hearer of the Word and not a doer, he is like a man who looks at his natural face in a mirror; for once he has looked at himself and gone away, he has immediately forgotten what kind of person he was. But one who looks intently at the perfect law, the law of liberty, and **abides by it**, not having become a **forgetful hearer** but an **effectual doer**, this man shall be **blessed in what he does**." James 1:23-25. I heard a preacher just recently ask by a show of hands how many people believed what they read in the newspaper. Hardly anyone raised a hand. Then he asked them how many believed that the Bible was true. Virtually everyone raised their hand. Then he said, "Why do you spend more time reading what you don't believe than what you do believe?"

Bridle his tongue. "If anyone thinks himself to be religious, and yet **does not bridle his tongue** but deceives his own heart, this man's religion is **worthless**." James 1:23-25. We just covered the importance of your wife being washed by the water of the Word. Do you read the Scriptures to *her* daily or ever? When was the last time you spewed unkind words at her? We must get control of our violent and hurtful tongues!

The savior. "For the **husband** is the head of the wife, as Christ also is the head of the church, He Himself being the Savior of the body." Eph. 5:23. **The husband is the Savior of the body**. Maybe you think your wife is to be the savior. When there is a financial crisis (or any crisis), it's the man who should "save the day." Don't encourage your wife to run out to get a job or make a financial plan. This is only robbing *you* of a blessing. Men, you must fulfill your role as the head of the home and the savior of the body. Pray for the Lord to bless you financially, and then turn around and bless your wife with your abundance.

Created to carry the burdens. You were created to carry the burdens of the family. Just look at your broad and muscular shoulders compared to your wife's shoulders. Women have even tried to imitate those shoulders with shoulder pads! Men are really designed to work best under pressure. Maybe you think you can't handle the pressures because you've always had your wife as your safety net.

A woman was created to handle many things at once. She has the home with each facet – each child, their various ages, personalities, needs; the meals, the cleaning, the continual tidying, the projects. Women seem like they can do it all. But while they are pretending to do it all, what are we doing? Sadly enough, we're usually playing sports or watching television.

Feeds us. You know that you are supposed to "bring home the bacon," but there is spiritual food that your children and your wife are literally starving for! "...for no one ever hated his own flesh, but nourishes and cherishes it, just as Christ also does the church...." Eph. 5:29. This feeding must be from "God's Word." Most men feel inadequate in this area. Many don't know where to begin. Pray to the Lord for strength and guidance daily! Satan will attack you in this area because he knows how important this area is to regaining leadership of your family. He will make you feel worthless, incapable, and downright stupid. *I know. He did with me!* He will use strife with your wife and children to stop your times of reading God's Word. Are you man enough to fight back in the spirit?

Begin to win one battle at a time to gain the momentum you need to become victorious in this area of your family's spiritual life. Don't just send them off to Bible studies, seminars, Sunday school and Vacation Bible School. To be an effective leader in your home, you must resist the temptation to give your leadership over to others. If you feel you don't have enough time, pray that God will show you where you should cut back and how you should feed your family **daily** from God's Word. Do it now. Pray just a short prayer, and then obey. It would be wise to write God's plan down on a piece of paper and put it in a place where you will continually see it.

Personal Commitment: To stop living treacherously with my wife. "Based on what I have learned in Scripture, I commit to renew my mind with the truth. I confess that I have lived with my wife in a treacherous way and I am seeking God for the power to change. I am also committing to washing my wife in the Word and to leading my family spiritually."

Date: _____ Signed: _____

————— Chapter 9 —————

Blessed Are the Meek

"Blessed are the meek,
For they shall inherit the earth."
Matthew 5:5

Meek is often regarded as weak. Yet Jesus told us "Blessed are the Meek"! The Webster's definition of meek is *humbly submissive*. In the concordance meek is defined as *gentle, humble, teachable and trainable*.

Sadly, husbands deal with their wives basically in one of two ways: they either treat them apathetically or they use the "tough love" approach. In this lesson we will search God's Word to find out the truth regarding love, humility, forgiveness and meekness.

True Love

Love is patient. God gives us a description of love. See if you can find the word "tough" or any word even remotely similar. "Love is **patient**, love is kind, and is not jealous; love does not brag and is not arrogant, does not act unbecomingly; it does not seek its own, is **not provoked, does not take into account a wrong suffered**, does not rejoice in unrighteousness, but rejoices with the truth; bears all things, believes all things, hopes all things, endures all things. Love never fails.... " 1Cor. 13:4-8.

I command you. Another very popular statement in the church today is "love is a choice." When Erin heard this, it was right at the time that she felt that she no longer wanted to love me; thankfully, she sought the Bible. Did God really say that she could "choose" to love me? Or, as she found out, that God *commands* us to love, as a follower of Christ? "This I **command** you, that you **love one another**." John 15:17. When ministering to others we tell those who don't want to love their unlovable spouse, "You do have a "choice": to obey His command or not."

Do good, bless, or pray for. Sometimes when our wife acts in an inappropriate way, especially if she pushes or manipulates us, we feel the need to "put her in her place". This is not the time to show her love, or is it? "But I say to you who hear, **love your enemies**, do good to those who hate you, bless those who curse you, pray for those who mistreat you." Luke 6:27-28. The Lord gave us only three choices when dealing with those we would rather be tough with: do good, bless, or pray for them.

Love your enemies. In this passage, God is even clearer. "But I say to you, **love your enemies**, and pray for those who persecute you...for if you love those who love you, what reward have you? Do not even the tax- gatherers do the same?" Matt. 5:44-46.

Overcome evil with good. "Rejoicing in hope, persevering in tribulation, devoted to prayer. Bless those who persecute you; bless and curse not. **Never pay back evil for evil to anyone**. Never take your own revenge, beloved, but leave room for the wrath of God, for it is written, 'Vengeance is Mine, I will repay,' says the Lord. But if your enemy is hungry, feed him, and if thirsty, give him a drink; for in doing so you will heap burning coals upon his head. Do not be overcome by evil, but **overcome evil with good**." Rom. 12:19.

Kept entrusting Himself. When you feel like lashing back at your wife and you don't, it can be very frustrating. Read God's explanation... "For you have been called for this purpose, since Christ also suffered for you, leaving you an example for you to follow in His steps...and while being reviled, **He did not revile in return**; while suffering, **He uttered no threats**, but kept entrusting Himself to Him [God] who judges righteously." 1Pet. 2:21-23.

They shall inherit the earth. If you don't take a "tough stand," others may call you a "wimp." However, let me remind you whom

Jesus said are "blessed." **"Blessed are the meek**, for they shall inherit the earth." Matt. 5:5.

You *may not* do the things that you please. When you have an impulse to do or say something to your wife that is anything but meek and loving, then you are walking in the flesh and are not walking in the Spirit. "But I say, walk in the Spirit, and you will not carry out the desire of the flesh. For the flesh sets its desire against the Spirit, and the Spirit against the flesh; for these are in opposition to one another, so that **you may not do the things that you please**. But the fruit of the Spirit is love, joy, peace, patience, kindness, goodness, faithfulness, gentleness, **self-control**." Gal. 5:16–23.

It's the kindness of God. Satan tries to deceive us into believing that confronting, being unkind and firm, will turn the other person around. If that worked, why would God use kindness to draw us to repentance? Sinners do not go to the altar to accept the Lord because they think that they are going to be criticized or chastised, do they? "Or do you think lightly of the riches of His kindness and forbearance and patience, not knowing that the **kindness of God** leads you to repentance?" Rom. 2:4.

Ministry of reconciliation. "Now all these things are from God, who reconciled us to Himself through Christ, and gave us the **ministry of reconciliation**, namely, that God was in Christ reconciling the world to Himself, not counting their trespasses against them, and He has committed to us the word of reconciliation. Therefore, we are **ambassadors** for Christ, as though God were entreating through us; we beg you on behalf of Christ, be reconciled to God." 2Cor. 5:18-20.

You who are spiritual. This Scripture is the measuring stick for our spirituality. Are you able to restore your wife in a spirit of gentleness? "Brethren, even if a man is caught in any trespass, you who are spiritual, **restore such a one in a spirit of gentleness**; each one looking to yourself, **lest you too be tempted**. Bear one another's burdens, and thus fulfill the law of Christ." Gal. 6:1-2. This Scripture warns us to be gentle toward others when they have sinned against us or we will be tempted in the same trespass.

Doers of the Word. It's important that we learn the truth and agree with what we see in Scripture, but we must not stop there: "But prove yourselves **doers of the word**, and not merely hearers who delude themselves...not having become a forgetful hearer but an effectual doer, this man shall be blessed in what he does." James. 1:22, 25. "Therefore, to him who **knows the right thing to do**, and does not do it, to him it is sin." James 4:17.

Forgiveness

Many men do not forgive their wives because they don't fully understand the grave consequences of their lack of forgiveness. Let's search the Scriptures to see what God says about forgiving others. Here are some questions we should ask:

Q. Why should I forgive?

Because God forgave us. "And be kind to one another, tender-hearted, forgiving each other, just as God in
Christ also has forgiven you." Eph. 4:32.

Because Jesus shed His blood. Jesus Christ shed His blood for the forgiveness of sins. "All things are cleansed with blood, and without the shedding of blood there is no forgiveness." Heb. 9:22. "For this is my blood of the covenant, which is poured out for many *for* **forgiveness of sins.**" Matt. 26:28.

Comfort her. To relieve the offender's sorrow: "...You should rather forgive and **comfort** him, lest somehow such a one be overwhelmed by excessive sorrow. Wherefore I urge you to **reaffirm your love** for him." 2Cor. 2:7-8. This really goes against our grain; it's so easy attack and to try to find fault with our wife, isn't it?

Are we ignorant of his schemes? "For if indeed what I have forgiven...I did it for your sakes in the presence of Christ, in order that **no advantage be taken of us by Satan**; for we are not ignorant of his schemes." 2Cor. 2:10-11. Don't allow Satan to take advantage of either of you.

Forgive her from your heart. God said that He would not forgive us unless *we* are willing to forgive others. "For if you forgive men for their transgressions, your heavenly Father will also forgive you, but if you do not forgive men, then your Father will **not forgive your transgressions**." Matt. 6:14-15. (Read all of Matt. 18: 22-35.)

Q. But shouldn't the offender be sorry before I forgive?

Father forgive them. Those who crucified Jesus **did not** ask for forgiveness; nor were they sorry for what they were doing or what they had done. We as Christians are to follow Jesus' example. **"Father forgive them, for they know not what they do."** Luke 23:34 KJV. When Stephen was being stoned, he cried out just before he died, "**Lord, do not hold this sin against them!**" Acts 7:60.

Q. But how often does God expect me to forgive another?

Seventy times seven. When Peter asked how often he was to forgive his brother, Jesus said to him, "I do not say to you, up to seven times, but up to **seventy times seven**." Matt. 18:22.

Inherit a blessing. We are all aware of what a monetary inheritance is. Here is a Spiritual inheritance God has called us to: "Not returning evil for evil, or insult for insult, but giving a blessing instead; for you were called for the very purpose that you might **inherit a blessing**." 1Pet. 3:9. Those who have ears let them hear this call.

Forget it. Does forgiveness really mean that I forget that sin, even during an argument? "For I will forgive their iniquity, and their sin I will **remember no more**." Jer. 31:34. "As far as the east is from the west, so far has He removed our transgressions from us." Ps. 103:12. Do you bring up things from the past? Don't allow satan to use you to condemn your wife or others who have received forgiveness by bringing up things from their past. But you say your wife does it all the time? You take the lead, you are the man, you need to be her protector not her accuser!

Q. How can I forgive as God has asked me to do in His Word?

Who can forgive sins? Only God can help you to do it. You must humble yourself and ask Him to give you the grace. "Who can forgive sins but God alone?" Mark 2:7.

Grace to the humble. How do I get the grace I need? "God is opposed to the proud but gives **grace to the humble**. Humble yourselves therefore under the mighty hand of God that He may exalt you at the proper time." 1Pet. 5:5-6.

Humbled. How can I gain humility? "Because they had rebelled against the Words of God. And spurned the counsel of the Most High. Therefore He **humbled** their heart **with labor**; they stumbled and there was none to help. Then they cried out to the Lord in their trouble; He saved them out of their distresses." Ps. 107:11-13. "I **humbled** my soul **with fasting**; and my **prayer** kept returning to my bosom." Ps 35:13. Sometimes it could be through illness that he quiets and humbles you. Don't fight it – God is working!

Go your way first. When do I need to forgive those who have hurt me? Shouldn't I feel convicted of it first? "If therefore you are presenting your offering at the altar, and there remember that your brother has something against you, leave your offering there before the altar, and go your way; *first* **be reconciled to your brother**, and then come and present your offering." Matt. 5:23-24. If you have not forgiven another, especially your wife, you need to ask forgiveness.

Put away. Not forgiving someone causes bitterness. The definition of bitterness is "poisonous!" "Let all **bitterness** and wrath and anger...be put away from you." Eph 4:31. Not forgiving another eats at *you*, not the other person! "The heart knows its own bitterness." Prov. 14:10. "For He knows the secrets of the heart." Ps. 44:21.

A brother offended. When you go to reconcile with your wife (or another person), be sure that you follow Scriptural guidelines. You may have heard those who have said that things were actually worse when they did ask forgiveness or that it did no good. Be sure that you speak with humility and sincerity, because if you ask for another's forgiveness in the wrong way, you may re-offend them. "A **brother offended** is harder to be won than a strong city." Prov. 18:19.

I have sinned. The Prodigal Son prepared his words after his decision to return home, "I will get up and go to my father, and will say to him, 'Father **I have sinned** against heaven, and in your sight; I am no longer worthy to be called your son; make me as one of your hired men.' " Luke 15:18-19.

Every idle word. Your words must be carefully chosen. "**Every idle word** that men shall speak they shall give an account thereof in the day of judgment." Matt. 12:36. Try writing down what you are going to say, then read **out loud** what you have written, putting yourself in the other person's shoes and hearing it from their point of view. Did it sound accusing? If so, ask God to put the right words in your mouth.

Many words. "When there are **many words**, transgression is unavoidable." Prov. 10:19. "A babbling fool will be thrown down." Prov. 10:10. Only mention what *you* did, don't set the stage with something like, "When you did this and such and such, well then I...."

He uttered no threats. "Agree with thine adversary quickly, while thou art in the way with him...." Matt. 5:25 KJV. If the other person starts to lash out at you, do not open your mouth except to agree. "And while being reviled, He did not revile in return; while suffering **He uttered no threats**...." 1Pet. 2:23.

Sweet to the soul. Make your words sweet and kind. "Sweetness of speech adds persuasiveness." Prov. 16:21. "Pleasant words are a honeycomb, **sweet to the soul** and healing to the bones." Prov. 16:24.

Revealing his own mind. Some men who have been guilty of infidelity in their past run to their wives for the purpose of relieving their own feelings of guilt. Be very aware of your wife's pain that will follow your confession. Don't use the excuse of repentance to dump your guilt on her. "A fool does not delight in understanding, but only in revealing his own mind." Prov. 18:2.

Confesses and forsakes. Confess to another Christian man your sin of adultery and make yourself accountable to him. "He who conceals his transgressions will not prosper, but he who **confesses and forsakes** them will find compassion." Prov. 28:13. If you are quite sure your wife already knows, suspects, or has confronted you about this sin, by all means confess.

Disgraceful. Just be discreet and leave the details out! Some women, desperately trying to relieve their pain, beg their husbands for details. Some men are foolish enough to comply, only multiplying the offenses toward her. "…for it is disgraceful even to speak of the things which are done by them in secret." Eph. 5:12. Love her enough to protect her.

Not be blotted out. Be prepared to reap what you have sown by comforting her and holding her up in her pain. Don't lash back with "you don't forgive" if she hurts or grieves for a long time. It may take years, or a lifetime, for her to recover from the hurt. Don't let this discourage you, but rather use it for good with the mindset that this will give you more opportunity to minister to her with love and patience. "The one who commits adultery with a woman is lacking sense; He who would destroy himself does it. Wounds and disgrace he will find, and his reproach will not be blotted out." Prov. 6:32-33.

Personal Commitment: To desire and strive to be meek. "Based on what I have learned in Scripture, I commit to practicing everything I have learned by being quick to hear and slow to speak: to forgive those who have offended me and to do what I can to reconcile with those I have offended."

Date:_____Signed: _____

Testimony

When Debbie* first met her husband Matt*, her mother told her that there was no way *he* could ever lead her. Her mother said, "Debbie, you are much too stubborn and pigheaded."

But after many years of marriage, the opposite was true. Matt, though very kind, extremely gentle and meek, had gained Debbie's admiration and respect. She said, "I just do whatever he says because I want to – and even when I don't want to, I do it anyway!" Debbie's husband obviously has many of the qualities of Christ: meekness, gentleness and goodness.

Those who followed after our Lord did so because he demonstrated God's love. Matt too has gained a following: Debbie.

*Not their real names.

───────── Chapter 10 ─────────

Desires of Your Heart

"The king's heart is like channels of water
in the hand of the Lord;
He turns it wherever He wishes."
Proverbs 21:1

Has everyone told you that your wife has her own will; therefore, she may "choose" not to return to you? When trying to restore your marriage you will be bombarded, as other men have, by the onslaught of those who will tell you that it is your wife's choice and her "free will" to choose to leave you or to be with another man. But, praise the Lord, this is not the truth!!

The key is not your wife's will, but **God's** will! And when seeking God's word it is clear to see that it is His will to turn your wife's heart back to you, her husband, because it is what He joined together. Glory to God!

It's NOT Man's Will but God's Will!!

"He does **His** *will*...." Dan. 4:31

"He bestows it on whomever **He** wishes...." Dan. 4:25

"**God** is able to deliver...." Dan 3:17

Consider Nebuchadnezzar. After his pride caused him to crawl like an animal, he said of God, "He does according to His will in the host of heaven and among the inhabitants of earth; And no one can ward off His hand or say to Him, 'What hast Thou done?'" Dan.

4:35. Is this not the same God who still does according to His will? Is your wife greater than King Nebuchadnezzar?

Consider also Jonah. Jonah was unwilling to do what God wanted him to do, but God *made* him willing. "And the Lord appointed a great fish to swallow Jonah, and Jonah was in the stomach of the fish three days and three nights." Jonah 1:17. God is MORE THAN ABLE to make your wife willing!

Lastly, consider Paul. "Now Saul, still breathing threats and murder against the disciples of the Lord…suddenly a light from heaven flashed around him…and Saul got up from the ground, and though his eyes were open, he could see nothing…the Lord Jesus…has sent me so that you may regain your sight and be filled with the Holy Spirit. And immediately there fell from his eyes something like scales, and he regained his sight, and he arose and was baptized." Acts 9:1-18.

God is MORE THAN ABLE to change your wife in an **instant**!! *I have seen it done countless times!* If you say "But you don't know my wife," I would say – you don't know God!!

Turning the Heart

As I mention earlier, you may hear some pastors and other Christians say that it is your wife's will to leave you, divorce you, or be with another man. But we just learned in Scripture that it is not man's will but God's will.

It may be your wife's will to leave you, divorce you, or be with someone else. Nevertheless, **God can turn her heart!**

You don't need to worry about her will. Instead you need to pray for your wife's heart to be turned. "The king's **heart** is like channels of water in the hand of the LORD; **He turns** it wherever He wishes." Prov. 21:1.

Pray that God will give your wife a new heart and replace her heart of stone with a heart of flesh! "Moreover, I will give you a **new**

heart and put a new spirit within you; and I will remove the heart of stone from your flesh and give you a **heart of flesh**." Ezek. 36:26.

The first step in turning your wife's heart is to find God's promises (His truths) and then meet the conditions of those promises. Here are several that we recommend you memorize:

"When man's ways are pleasing to the Lord, He makes even his enemies to be at peace with him." Prov. 16:7

"Delight yourself in the Lord and He will give you the desires of your heart." Ps. 37:4

"Commit your way to the Lord, trust also in Him and He will do it." Ps. 37:5

"Seek first the kingdom of God and His righteousness and all these things will be added unto you." Matt. 6:33

Remember you need to put God first in your life; He never wants to be second place to anything or anyone. Once He is first, you will begin to be transformed into His image. That is when you will begin to see your wife's heart turn back to you.

If you struggle with this principle of man's will versus God's will, you will need to renew your mind with the verses in this chapter to overcome the doubts of "man's will theology" and replace it with God's focus, which is the **heart**!

Let's look at the Scriptures that tell us how God changed the hearts of men and even kings:

"He put this in the king's heart...." Ezra 7:27-28.

"He hardened the hearts of the Egyptians...." Exodus 14:17.

"The Lord hardened Pharaoh's heart...." Exodus 10:27.

"The Lord turns the heart wherever He wishes...." Prov. 21:1.

In the book of Proverbs we learn wisdom. Proverbs 1 verses 2 through 7 lists the benefits of Proverbs:

To know wisdom.
To receive instruction.
To receive instruction in wise behavior.
Also instruction in righteousness, justice and equity.
Prudence to the naive. To the youth knowledge.

Read Proverbs every day for wisdom! (Go to our website "Daily Devotional" for the verses to read every day.)

Wives Who Are Unwilling

Not all wives return home even after God turns their hearts. Many wives, unfortunately, go against their hearts because their husbands are the same men they chose to leave. Once again, God is MORE THAN ABLE to turn your wife's heart back to you. But, if you are still impatient, unkind and proud, then once her heart turns toward you, the OLD you will cause her to harden her heart and make a mental decision rather than a heart decision!

Make sure you read and reread this book over and over again! Make sure you live in the Word. Make sure you spend hours daily with your face to the ground, seeking His face. You must be a new man for your wife to want to follow her heart and come home! Remember, the reason your wife has left or has gotten caught by an adulter is because your home was not built on the rock of Jesus Christ.

Let's look at Proverbs and some New Testament Scriptures:

House of the proud. "The Lord will tear down the **house of the proud**." Prov. 14:1.

House divided against itself. "Any kingdom or house divided against itself is laid waste: and any city or **house divided against itself** shall not stand...." Matt. 12:25.

Yet it did not fall. "Therefore, everyone who hears these words of Mine, and acts upon them, may be compared to a wise man, who built his house upon the rock. And the rain descended, and the floods came, and the winds blew, and burst against that house; and **yet it did not fall**, for it had been founded upon the rock." Matt. 7:24-25.

Built together. "…Christ Jesus being the cornerstone, in whom the whole building, being fitted together, is growing into a holy temple in the Lord; in whom you also are being **built together** into a dwelling of God in the Spirit…." Eph. 2:21.

Let no man separate. "And He answered and said, 'Have you not read, that He who created them from the beginning made them male and female, and said, "for this cause a man shall leave his father and mother, and shall cleave to his wife; and the two shall become one flesh"? Consequently they are no longer two, but one flesh. What therefore God has joined together, **let no man separate**." Matt. 19:4-6.

God has promised to heal, restore and create praise on your lips! "Because of the iniquity of his unjust gain I was angry and struck him; I hid My face and was angry, And he went on turning away, in the way of his heart. I have seen his ways, but I will **heal** him; I will lead him and **restore** comfort to him and to his mourners, creating the **praise** of the lips. Peace, peace to him who is far and to him who is near, says the Lord, and I will heal him." Isa. 57:17-19.

You must seek the Lord to break and change you if it is your desire to have your wife care for you again. (See *A Wise Man Builds Upon A Rock: By a FOOL Who Tore His Down with His Own Hands* for help.)

NOTHING is impossible for God!
The Lord Turns the Heart Wherever HE Wishes!

Personal commitment: to ask God to turn my wife's heart and not to fear the will of man. "Based on what I have learned in Scripture, I commit to trusting the Lord to turn my wife's heart. I dispel the lie that says 'my wife has a free will; therefore, God will not intervene on my behalf and answer my prayers.' Instead, I believe that my 'wife's will' will follow after God turns her heart back home."

Date: _____ Signed:_____

Chapter 11

Cleave to His Wife

" 'For I hate divorce,'
says the Lord, the God of Israel."
Malachi 2:16

Why are so many marriages ending in divorce? We have all heard the statistics...50% of **first** marriages end in divorce and 80% of **second** marriages end in divorce. That means that only 20% of second marriages survive! The real shame is that just as many marriages end in divorce IN the church!! Christians now accept divorce as an option! Why the onslaught of failed marriages?

"And the rain descended, and the floods came, and the winds blew, and burst against that house; and yet it did not fall, **for it had been founded upon the rock**." Matt. 7:25. Was your house built on the Rock? "And the rain descended, and the floods came, and the winds blew, and burst against that house; and it fell, and **great was its fall**." Matt. 7:27.

The Rock we need to build on is the Word of God! How many of us really knew the principles that you have read in this book thus far concerning marriage? Hos. 4:6 tells us that "we are perishing for a lack of knowledge." This was certainly true for me and I am sure it is true for you too!

So then when our marriage fails, we seek to be released from the marriage only to repeat the mistakes in the second or subsequent marriage. God hates divorce, but when we are in the midst of trouble that's what we believe will bring us relief. We even try to convince ourselves and others that divorce is what God wants for us since He wouldn't want us to suffer.

The Deception

When we entertain a wrong thought or idea, God tells us: "Each one is tempted when he is carried away and enticed by his **own lust**. (The definition of lust is a "longing" for what is forbidden, like longing for a divorce when God says "I hate divorce.") Then when lust has conceived, it gives birth to sin; and when sin is accomplished, it brings forth death. Do not be deceived, my beloved brethren." Jas 1:14-16. Many say that there is nothing wrong with divorce, especially in certain circumstances.

We must obey God rather than man. Everyone has his or her own opinion concerning marriage and divorce (what he or she "thinks" God tells us pertaining to marriage in His Word). But, "We must **obey God** rather than man." Acts 5:29.

He is our only hope for salvation. Don't follow what another person says. Instead, follow God; obey Him, for *He* is our only hope for salvation. Don't complicate His Word by trying to find "what you *think* He means." **He means exactly what He says!**

I am not ashamed of the gospel of Christ. Please stand by God's teachings regardless of what is popular or how many people in your church have divorced and/or remarried. "I am not ashamed of the gospel of Christ, for it is the power of God for salvation to everyone who believes." Rom. 1:16.

Please understand that if marriages are to be saved, we must stand on truth! Those second marriages that "seem" happy are in fact living in defeat, not a testimony of God's faithfulness. They continue to cause many others to suffer or live at less than God's best, especially the children who suffer the most! And they cause many to stumble who are experiencing difficulty in their marriages. It is very tempting to want to find a second wife when many profess that they found happiness in their second marriage after they finally got rid of their first wife!

With gentleness correcting those who are in opposition. Please do not debate the issue of divorce. Each person is only responsible to speak, teach, and live the truth. Then the Holy Spirit will do the convicting, and the Lord will turn the heart. "But refuse foolish and ignorant speculations, knowing that they produce quarrels. s And the Lord's bond-servant must not be quarrelsome, but be kind to all, able to teach, patient when wronged, with **gentleness correcting** those who are in opposition, if perhaps God may grant them repentance leading to the knowledge of the truth, and they may come to their senses and escape from the snare of the devil, having been held captive by him to do his will." 2Tim. 2:23-26.

The tree is known by its fruit. We can see the "fruits" of many of those in church leadership – those who have allowed the widespread abuse of "exceptions" for divorce. We have seen that it began with the loophole of "unfaithfulness or adultery" and has led to divorce for practically any reason! It parallels what has happened with the abortion issue...rape, incest, and the health of the mother now account for less than 1% of all abortions performed! "You will know them by their **fruits**." Matt. 7:16. "Either make the tree good, and its fruit good; or make the tree bad, and its fruit bad; for the tree is known by its fruit." Matt. 12:33. We can clearly see the bad fruit that has been produced by compromising God's Word – broken marriages and broken vows.

The Questions

Why must we understand and follow God's Law concerning marriage?

Because families are being destroyed, and without the family, the foundation on which our country stands will have been removed, and great will be our fall! We, as Christians, will be to blame. We cannot point the finger at others because God promises us as believers that if "My people who are **called by My name** will humble themselves and pray and seek My face and turn from their wicked ways, then I will hear from heaven, will forgive their sin, and will *heal* their land." 2Chron. 7:14.

Yet, Christian marriages are perishing at the same rate of destruction as those in the world. Why? "My people perish for a lack of knowledge." Hos. 4:6. Christians have been deceived, and are following the world's ways rather than God's ways.

How can we know that we are being deceived about marriage and divorce?

Turning aside to myths. Many of those who sit in the church pews don't want to hear the truth. "For the time will come when they will not endure sound doctrine; but wanting to have their ears tickled, they will accumulate for themselves teachers in accordance to their own desires and will turn away their ears from the truth, and will turn aside to myths." 2Tim 4:3-4.

We now seek worldly solutions for troubled or wounded marriages rather than seeking the Lord and His Word. "But you are a chosen generation, a royal priesthood, a holy nation, a *peculiar* people." 1Pet. 2:9. We are not a "peculiar people" if we just follow the beaten path that leads to the divorce court!

You may not do the things you please. His Word is always consistent; God's Word is opposed to the world's philosophies and sometimes difficult to understand and follow. "But a natural man does not accept the things of the Spirit of God; they are foolishness to him, and he cannot understand them, because they are spiritually appraised." 1Cor. 2:14. "But I say, walk by the Spirit, and you will not carry out the desire of the flesh...so you may not do the things that you please." Gal. 5:17.

Bad fruit. Again, we can easily see "the fruits" of all the Christian marriages that have been destroyed because they believed the lies. "You will know them by their fruits. Grapes are not gathered from thorn bushes, nor figs from thistles, are they? Even so, every good tree bears good fruit; but the bad tree bears **bad fruit**." Matt. 7:15-17.

Scriptural Facts to Stand On

Let's search more Scriptures to see how God views marriage.

Marriage is for life. We say the vows *until **death** do we part.* "Consequently they are no longer two but one flesh. What therefore God has joined together, let no man separate." Matt. 19:6. "AND THE TWO SHALL BECOME ONE FLESH; consequently they are no longer two, but one flesh." Mark 10:8.

God says that He hates divorce! Yet, some men are actually convinced that God led them to get a divorce! Some have said that God has "released me." **He says**... "For I hate divorce says the Lord." Malachi 2:16. He never changes... "Jesus Christ is the same yesterday and today, yes and forever." Heb. 13:8.

You are not the exception: "I most certainly understand that God is not One to show partiality." Acts 10:34.

Remarriage is not an "option" – the Bible says it's "adultery"! "...**but I say** [Jesus Himself said] to you that everyone who divorces his wife, except for the cause of unchastity, makes her commit adultery; and whoever marries a divorced woman **commits adultery**." Matt. 5:32. "And I say to you, whoever **divorces his *wife*,** except for immorality (fornication, KJV), and marries another woman **commits adultery**." Matt. 19:9.

Commits adultery. "And **He** [Jesus again] said to them, 'Whoever **divorces his *wife*** and marries another woman **commits adultery** against her....'" Mark 10:11. "Everyone who **divorces his *wife*** and marries another **commits adultery;** and he who marries one who is divorced from a husband **commits adultery**." Luke 16:18.

Lacking sense. "The one who commits adultery with a woman is **lacking sense**; he who would destroy himself does it." Prov. 6:32. "If there is a man who commits adultery with another man's wife, one who commits adultery with his friend's wife, the adulterer and the adulteress shall surely be put to death." Lev. 20:10.

What about the "exception" clause?

Again, very few divorces in the church are for the reason of adultery, even if that were the correct "exception." When Erin was told that she had grounds for divorce because I was in adultery, she sought to find out the truth. What she found was that is many Bible translations the words "adultery" and "fornication" or "moral impurities" were used **interchangeably** as though they were the same words – but she found they are not the same words! The word "adultery" (Strong's Concordance in the Greek or original language is 3429 *Moichao*) that means an act if intimacy *after* marriage. But the word "fornication" (4202) means and act of intimacy *before* marriage. Therefore these are two separate sins and should not be confused.

So when the Bible says in Matt. 19:9 "And I say to you, whoever divorces his wife, **except** for *immorality*, and marries another woman commits adultery." This exception meant that a man could divorce his wife if before they were married she was found to have been immoral or committed fornication as was the case with Joseph when the Bible said he contemplated divorcing her secretly (Matt. 1:19). It is NOT saying that if you find that your wife has committed adultery, which is intimacy after marriage, that you can divorce your wife.

With this information, we could rewrite the verse in Matthew with the correct translation to say: "...**but I** [Jesus] **say** that everyone who divorces his wife, makes her commit adultery; and whoever marries a divorced woman **commits adultery.**" Only when a **woman** was found *on or before* her wedding day not to be a virgin, only then could the husband divorce his wife. And again, Moses only allowed men to divorce: "Because of your hardness of heart, Moses permitted you to divorce your wives; but from the beginning it has not been this way." Matt. 19:8. In other words, NO, you cannot divorce your wife since the *exception* clause does not apply to *after* marriage.

Be careful when you say that "God told you"! "Behold, I am against those who use their tongues and declare 'The Lord declares.' Behold, I am against those who have prophesied false dreams, declares the Lord, and related them and led my people astray by their falsehoods and reckless boasting." Jer. 23:31-32. "For I **hate** divorce, says the Lord." Malachi 2:16. God never tells us to go against His Word! He never changes! Never!! You also must be very careful what you say about divorce or remarriage since it could lead another person to stumble and divorce or remarry: "Woe to the world because of its stumbling blocks! For it is inevitable that stumbling blocks come; but woe to that man through whom the stumbling block comes!...It is better for him that a heavy millstone be hung around his neck, and that he be drowned in the depth of the sea." Matt. 18:7,6.

Many have been deceived. If you believe that God wants the divorce, you have been deceived. "And no wonder, for even Satan disguises himself as an angel of light." 2Cor. 11:14.

Flesh reaps corruption. "For the one who sows to his own flesh shall from the flesh reap corruption, but the one who sows to the Spirit shall from the Spirit reap eternal life." Gal. 6:8. Check to see how "driven" you are before you go step out in faith. Fleshly desires feel good to the flesh; if you have urgency behind it, you need no grace to carry it out. "For the flesh sets its desire against the Spirit, and the Spirit against the flesh; for these are in opposition to one another, so that you may not do the things that you please." Gal. 5:17.

God and only God! What knowledge has been gained from seeing so many broken and troubled marriages? God and only God can save and keep a marriage together; though your obedience to His Word. But you have to know His Word before you can begin to obey it. "My people perish for a lack of knowledge." Hosea 4:6. That's why you MUST read the chapters in this book over and over and over again! That's why you must meditate on His Word. That's why you must feed on His Word not just every day, but all day long!

**Let us make a personal commitment to
REMAIN MARRIED
and encourage all we encounter to do the same.**

Personal commitment: to remain married and encourage others to do the same. "Based on what I have learned from God's Word, I recommit myself to my marriage. I will humble myself when necessary and take all steps as a 'peacemaker' in my marriage. I will not cover my transgressions nor cause another to stumble. I will devote my lips to spreading God's Truth on marriage."

Date: _____ Signed: _____

— Chapter 12 —

Ask of God

"But if any of you lacks wisdom,
let him ask of God,
who gives to all men generously
and without reproach,
and it will be given to him."
James 1:5

What if my wife is unfaithful and commits adultery, am I then allowed to divorce her?

No! As we just learned in Chapter 11 "Cleave to His Wife" God's Word says that a *husband* could divorce for the reason of **fornication** only (which is intercourse prior to marriage) if the *woman* was defiled. no matter what your Bible translation may seem to say. **The only exception refers to the time of betrothal only.** Fornication and adultery are not the same sin. If they were, these sins would not be stated *twice* in the same Scripture verse: "...neither **fornicators**, idolaters, nor **adulterers**...." 1Cor. 6:9.

Divorce her secretly. Divorce for the cause of fornication was allowed during the betrothal time, as in the case of Mary and Joseph. The terms fiancé and engagement were not used during this period of history. The term "husband" was used because Joseph had already committed to being Mary's husband. "And Joseph, her husband...desired to **divorce her secretly**." Matt. 1:19. This was prior to their marriage because divorce was allowed for the case of fornication only.

Betrothed. The previous verse explains that the "divorce" was to take place **before** the marriage! "...Mary had been **betrothed** to Joseph, **before** they came together she was found to be with child...."

Matt. 1:18. The latest a divorce could take place was immediately after the wedding night, if the woman was found not to be a virgin.

Can anyone then ever remarry?

"A wife is bound as long as her husband lives; but if her husband is dead, **she is free to be married** to whom she wishes, only in the Lord." 1Cor. 7:39. For those women who are widowed, it is important to know that when the real "Mr. Right" comes along he too will be widowed or will never have been married. Remember, Satan usually brings his best first, but the Lord makes you wait and then brings His best! "Wait for the Lord, and keep His way." Ps. 37:34.

What if I am already in a second (or third) marriage?

First, you must ask God's forgiveness, whether you were married before you were saved or not. You can't be effective in your Christian walk if you can't admit past sins. "He who covers his transgressions shall not prosper." Prov. 28:13. "If we say that we have no sin, we are deceiving ourselves, and the truth is not in us. If we confess our sins, He is **faithful** and **righteous** to **forgive us our sins** and to cleanse us from **all** unrighteousness." 1John 1:8-9.

Time to repent. "Therefore, confess your sins to one another, and pray for one another, so that you may be healed. The effective prayer of a righteous man can accomplish much." Jas. 5:16.

Should I restore this marriage or go back to my first wife?

His will. After you confess your sin of getting ahead of God by remarrying or marrying someone who was already married, you must lay *your* **will** aside and ask your Heavenly Father for *His* **will** concerning your present marriage. Does the Lord want you to continue to seek restoration for this marriage that is falling apart? Many men have faced this difficult task, but God is ALWAYS faithful and He will guide you if you seek Him. Pray for God's direction. "The thief comes only to steal, and kill, and destroy; I came that they might have life, and might have it abundantly." John 10:10.

We are no longer under the law, but live under grace when we accept the gift of salvation. God may want to restore your first marriage, or your second marriage or maybe He would rather you live a life of singleness. God has an abundant life for you, but only as you desire His will can you find it. If you continue to seek your own will, wanting your first marriage or your current marriage or a new marriage, you will continually live in misery and defeat. Seek Him and His will for you. "'For I know the plans that I have for you,' declares the LORD, 'plans for welfare and not for calamity to give you a future and a hope.'" Jer. 29:11.

What's the truth about "Covenant Marriages". The fact is that God DOES recognize second marriages. The term "covenant marriage" was coined from Mal. 2:14: "Yet you say, 'For what reason?' Because the Lord has been a witness between you and the wife of your youth, against whom you have dealt treacherously, though she is your companion and your wife by covenant." It does not say that it is a first marriage or that a first marriage is all that the Lord will recognize. We cannot read into a verse to make it say what we WANT it to say. "For the time will come when they will not endure sound doctrine; but *wanting* to have their ears tickled, they will accumulate for themselves teachers in accordance to their own desires; and will turn away their ears from the truth, and will turn aside to myths." 2Tim. 4:3-4. Only the truth will set us free.

Ignoring or minimizing the power of Christ's shed blood. When you believe that God will NOT forgive a second or subsequent marriage, but sees it only as ongoing adultery, you are saying that Jesus' blood is unable to cover the sin of adultery caused by divorcing and remarrying.

But this verse tells us differently: "Or do you not know that the unrighteous shall not inherit the kingdom of God? Do not be deceived; neither fornicators, nor idolaters, nor *adulterers*…shall inherit the kingdom of God. And such **WERE some of you**; but you were washed, but you were sanctified, but you were justified in the name of the Lord Jesus Christ, and in the Spirit of our God." 1Cor. 6:9. Hallelujah! God can and does forgive adultery, any and all adultery! "And Jesus said, 'Neither do I condemn you; go your way. From now on sin no more.' " John 8:11.

Trust Him. If you want the abundant life God has for you as one of His children, you must trust Him with your life. God wants to give you an abundant life, not a counterfeit. If you choose to try and do this yourself, it is in vain. Ps. 127:1 says, "Unless the Lord builds the house, they labor in vain who build it…."

Can adultery be forgiven?

Yes. Jesus said to the woman caught in adultery: "Did no one condemn you? ... Neither do I condemn you; go your way. From now on sin no more." John 8:10-11. Actually, not only is **adultery** NOT grounds for divorce, it is **grounds for forgiveness** as Christ showed in John 8:10 above.

We also have an example in Hosea of a spouse forgiving adultery in Hos. 3:1. "Then the Lord said to me, 'Go again, love a woman who is loved by her husband, yet an adulteress.' " Then in 1Cor. 6:9-11, when God refers to adulterers and fornicators, He says: "And such **were** some of you; but you were washed, but you were sanctified, but you were justified in the name of the Lord Jesus Christ, and in the Spirit of our God." We are washed in His blood of forgiveness.

Yet, too many pastors say that adultery is grounds for divorce. "You have heard that it was said, 'You shall not commit adultery'; but I say to you that everyone who *looks* on a woman to lust for her has committed adultery with her already in his heart." Matt. 5:27-28. If it were true that adultery was grounds for divorce, then most women could divorce their husbands since most of us have lusted over pictures of women on television or in magazines!

If you have committed adultery, you must confess your sin to your wife if she is unaware of your unfaithfulness. "He who conceals his transgressions will not prosper, but he who confesses and forsakes them will find compassion." Prov. 28:13.

Isn't remarriage okay if it's under the right circumstances?

Again, we believe that too many churches and pastors say that divorce is right in *some* situations, but this verse clearly says, "Whoever then annuls one of the least of these commandments, and so teaches others, shall be called least in the kingdom of heaven; but whoever keeps and teaches them, he shall be called great in the kingdom of heaven." Matt. 5:19. Therefore, we, as teachers of the word will not annul, in other words, say that the verses about divorce are not valid.

How can I be sure that what **this** book says is right and what many of the churches are saying is wrong? The Scriptures warn us to "Beware of the false prophets, who come to you in sheep's clothing, but inwardly are ravenous wolves. Many will say to Me on that day, 'Lord, Lord, did we not prophesy in Your name, and in Your name cast out demons, and in Your name perform many miracles?' And then I will declare to them, 'I never knew you; Depart from Me, you who practice lawlessness.' " Matt. 7:15-23. Aren't many of the marriages in your church crumbling and the families dissolving? These, we believe, are the bad fruits from allowing divorce within the church.

I have found in talking to pastors about this issue that many of them personally feel a "deep down" conviction about marriage, but don't want to "offend" anyone, especially all those "church members" who are in their second and third marriages. Sadly, one who did finally take a stand in his church was met with a church division from those who were in second and subsequent marriages. They did not appreciate their pastor taking this firm stand on divorce and remarriage! However, when faced with making a decision, we must remember, "Friendship with the world is hostility toward God. Therefore whoever wishes to be a friend of the world makes himself an enemy of God." Jas. 4:4.

Ears tickled. If a pastor or church takes a stand against divorce and remarriage, they are labeled legalistic or judgmental. And those who want to "do their own thing" will go to another church to hear what they want to hear (to have their ears tickled). "For the time will come when they will not endure sound doctrine; but wanting to have their **ears tickled**, they will accumulate for themselves teachers in accordance to their own desires; and will turn away from the truth, and will turn aside to myths." 2Tim. 4:3-4.

Since I'm already divorced or single again, couldn't I remarry or at least date and then ask God to forgive me?

First of all, **you are not really single.** Only someone who has *never* been married (or a widow or widower) is single. Secondly, you will reap what you have sown. "Do not be deceived, God is not mocked; for whatever a man sows, this he will reap also." Gal. 6:7. You are willfully entering into sin. "Therefore to one who knows the right thing to do and does not do it, to him it is sin." Jas. 4:17.

A terrifying thing. You'll set yourself up for God's vengeance. "For if we go on sinning willfully after receiving the knowledge of the truth, there no longer remains a sacrifice for sins. How much more **severe a punishment** do you think he will deserve who has trampled under foot the Son of God. Vengeance is mine, I will repay. The Lord will judge His people. *It is a **terrifying thing** to fall into the hands of the living God."* Heb. 10:26-31. God will not be mocked. You will not benefit from ignoring God's Word, nor by trading obedience for a "better marriage" (or relationship) with someone new.

If You Love Me

In closing, "If anyone advocates a different doctrine and does not agree with sound words, those of our Lord Jesus Christ, and with the doctrine conforming to godliness, he is conceited and understands nothing; but has a morbid interest in controversial questions and disputes about words, out of which arise envy, strife, abusive language, evil suspicions, and constant friction between men of truth." 1Tim. 6:3-5. "If you love Me, you will keep My commandments." John 14:15. If you say you believe God, **then obey Him**. "Why do you call me Lord and not do what I say?" Luke 6:46. If you have decided to ask Jesus for your salvation but are not following His teachings, then He is not your Lord and Master. If He *is* your Lord, then be sure that you act like it. Obey Him!

Let us make a personal commitment to
SEEK THE LORD
and encourage all others to do the same!

Personal commitment: to seek the Lord as to whether I am to restore my present marriage. "Based on what I have learned from God's Word, I commit to ask God whether or not I am to restore this marriage. I will lay aside my will, wanting only His will since He is my Lord. I will never judge anyone who is in a second or subsequent marriage, but acknowledge that the blood of Jesus is able to cover the sin of adultery."

Date:_____Signed:_____

Chapter 13

He Guides Me

"And His name will be called
Wonderful Counselor,
Mighty God,
Eternal Father,
Prince of Peace."
Isaiah 9:6

My wife is filing for divorce; what should I do?
How do I find someone to defend me?
How can I protect myself and especially my children?

People who know about your situation may have been advising you to get a good Christian lawyer to protect you, your assets, and your children. It could be a Christian friend, a counselor or even your pastor. When I was divorcing Erin, she said that's when she found the "Mighty Counselor!" This is what she found in her Bible when she was searching for what God had to say on this subject. These are the principles she has shared with countless others who found that following these principles turned their situation around and brought peace where there once was war.

It shall not approach you. "And if anyone wants to sue you and take your shirt, let him have your coat also." Matt. 5:38-48. You may be worried that our wife will "take you to the cleaners" if you don't retain an attorney. But if you act like she's your enemy and fight, she'll fight back. Hasn't she in the past?

Many people share their "horror stories" about someone they knew lost everything to frighten you into getting a good lawyer. Just remember, "A thousand may fall at your side, and ten thousand at your right hand, but **it shall not approach you**." Ps. 91:7. Instead, "Do not be overcome by evil, but overcome evil with good." Rom. 12:21. Based on what Erin went through and the others who have followed this same path towards peace, we advise anyone who wants to restore their marriage to **release** their attorney and trust God ALONE to deliver and protect them.

Dare go before the unrighteous versus saints? "Does any one of you, when he has a case against his neighbor, dare to go to law before the unrighteous, and not before the saints?" 1Cor. 6:1. This is a very firm Scripture. Would you dare God? If you merely show up in court, you are standing "before the unrighteous."

In most states you would not violate the law if you didn't show up in court if you were served with divorce papers. You merely lose by default. Some states make you sign a waiver that you will not appear, and in others you must neither sign the papers nor show up. Check it out and don't just take one person's word for it if they tell you you "have to" do anything. (Our *Facing Divorce* book will help you with many of your questions.)

Rather be wronged or defrauded. This was one of the first verses the Lord showed Erin when she realized that she would be losing everything she wanted if she didn't fight me in court. "Actually, then, it is already a defeat for you, that you have lawsuits with one another. Why not rather be **wronged**? Why not rather be **defrauded**? On the contrary, you yourselves wrong and defraud, and that your brethren." 1Cor. 6:7-8. God says it is better that you are wronged and defrauded (cheated or tricked).

If you don't allow yourself to be wronged, your wife will end up angry and bitter. If you don't allow yourself to be backed up to the Red Sea, you will never see God's power of deliverance! Remember that the "cares and riches of the world will choke the Word!" (Matt. 13:22)

We are told through Scripture that Demas left Paul because the cares of the world choked the Word from him. The following verse tells us how... "And the one on whom seed was sown among the thorns, this is the man who hears the word, and the **worry** of the world and the deceitfulness of **riches** choke the word, and it becomes unfruitful." Matt. 13:22. Scripture says specifically that it was because of "worry" and because of "riches." Don't worry about or get caught up with money or possessions. What it really comes down to is this, are your possessions worth more than your wife and your marrriage?

We shall judge angels. "Or do you not know that the saints will judge the world? And if the world is judged by you, are you not competent to constitute the smallest law courts? Do you not know that **we shall judge angels**? How much more, matters of this life?" 1Cor. 6:2-3. God is mocking us, showing us how petty and insignificant the matters of this world are in comparison to our life with Him.

Matters of this life. "If then you have law courts **dealing with matters of this life**, do you appoint them as judges who are of no account in the church?" 1Cor. 6:4. The courts today do not follow Biblical teachings as they did when this country was founded. As a result, we have rulings and burdens placed upon believers that neither God nor our founding fathers had in mind. If you choose the courts to help you, you will choose *their* judgment over God's protection and provisions.

Before unbelievers. "I say this to your shame. Is it so, that there is not among you one wise man who will be able to decide between his brethren, but brother goes to law with brother, and that **before unbelievers**?" 1Cor. 6:5.

A defeat for you. Don't get a lawyer. If you have one, dismiss him or her. "Actually, then it is already **a defeat for you**, that you should have lawsuits with one another. Why not rather be wronged? Why not rather be defrauded?" 1Cor. 6:7. If you go into court with your spouse, it is already a defeat for you. You may get the terms and conditions that are written in the divorce papers, but you will lose your wife!

No one will see the Lord. "Pursue peace with all men, and sanctification without which **no one will see the Lord**." Heb. 12:14-15. If you wish to act as Jesus acted (who was totally innocent) remember that He "opened not His mouth in defense," 1Pet. 2:23. God can begin to work in your wife's life because you are planting seeds of life and no longer giving Satan fuel for destruction (see 1Pet. 3:1).

We want our wives to see Jesus' ways in us. We quench the work of the Holy Spirit when we do the things we "want to" instead of what we "ought to." Do it **God's way**!

Put away. "Let all bitterness, wrath and anger and clamor and slander be **put away** with all malice." Eph. 4:31. If you have a lawyer, slander and wrath WILL take place. This is what divorce is all about. You must put it away from you. It doesn't matter if you have a "Christian" attorney or not – all "**deliverance by *man* is in vain**"! "O, give us help against the adversary, for **deliverance by man is in vain**." Ps. 108:12-13.

You have this promise from God: "When a man's ways [*your* ways] are pleasing to the Lord, He makes even his enemies to be at peace with him." Prov. 16:7.

Take refuge in the Lord. "It is better to **take refuge in the Lord** than to trust in man." Ps. 118:8. A lawyer is no substitute for the Lord. If you think you can have both a lawyer and God's protection the following verse explains that they are opposing one another. "Cursed is the man who trusts in mankind and makes flesh his strength. Blessed is the man who trusts in the Lord and **whose trust IS the Lord**." Jer. 17:5-8. We have found that you can either be blessed or cursed. You must decide. Erin decided that she really could only trust the Lord and He delivered her because of her faith in trusting Him alone.

Cease striving. "**Cease striving** and know that I am God." Ps. 46:8-10. Put it in His hands. Stop wringing your hands about it; stop discussing it with everyone. Be still! If your wife has already begun divorce proceedings, and you have already humbled yourself and turned from your wicked ways, then follow these steps:

Called us to peace. Tell your wife that you do not want the divorce, but that you will not stand in her way (Ps. 1:1) and that you will NOT contest the divorce either. Tell her that you don't "blame her" for wanting to divorce you. Tell her that you will still love her (if the "hate wall" is down), no matter what she chooses to do. "Yet if the unbelieving one leaves, let him leave…but God has **called us to peace**." 2Cor. 7:15.

Sweetness of speech. Again, be sure to tell your wife that you will not contest or fight her in the divorce and that you won't get a lawyer for yourself. (If you have a lawyer, tell your wife that you will dismiss him or her.) Tell your wife that you trust her and know from her past that she will be fair, and that she will do what she believes is right for you and your children. The only way to win the war that is raging against your marriage is with kindness! "**Sweetness of speech** adds persuasiveness." Prov. 6:24.

I hate divorce. Tell your wife that you have made so many mistakes in the past that you don't want to make any more (humility in action). You hope that she will allow you NOT to sign the divorce papers because you have made so many mistakes. Seek the Lord for how He wants to deliver you and the words that He wants you to speak to your wife.

Remember, the Lord said, "**I hate divorce**." Of course if she persists in your signing, agree to sign and then pray diligently that the Lord will stop her from pursuing you to sign. If you are not the same disagreeable man that you were, and your wife sees a humble and meek husband, then she will not continue to press. Don't offer suggestions to try and please your wife; this is displeasing to the Lord. Seek the Lord!

Nothing is impossible. However, if you have participated in the divorce procedure, all is not lost. Ask the Lord's forgiveness and your wife's forgiveness also. Demonstrate your desire to have the family together by dropping any and all legal action or protection. God will begin to heal right now: "*With God* **nothing is impossible**." Matt 19:26.

Again, if you have retained a lawyer, dismiss him or her immediately if you want the Best to defend you. Then pray, "Lord, there is no one besides Thee to help us in the battle between the powerful and those who have no strength; so help us, O Lord our God, for we trust in Thee, and in Thy name have come against this, O Lord, Thou art our God; let not man prevail against Thee." 2Chron. 14:11.

Harder to be won. If you have already been through a divorce, bitterness and resentment and extreme anger are probably what your wife feels toward you now. Pray that God will forgive your transgressions and blot out the bad memories she has (Ps. 9:5) and replace them with good thoughts. Pray harder and be kinder (again, sweetness of speech adds persuasiveness) at every opportunity that you may have with your wife to win her back. Remember, "A brother offended is **harder to be won** than a strong city, and contentions are like the bars of a castle." Prov. 18:19.

Then I could bear it. God does understand what you are going through. Read some of Ps. 55; He's speaking directly to you. Beginning in verse 6, "Oh that I had wings like a dove! I would fly away and be at rest. Behold, I would wander far away, I would lodge in the wilderness. I would hasten to my place of refuge, from the stormy wind and tempest." Vs. 12-14: "For it is not an enemy who reproaches me, **then I could bear it**; nor is it one who hates me who exalted himself against me, then I could hide myself from him. But it is you, a man my equal, my companion and my familiar friend, we who had sweet fellowship together...."

Steal, and kill, and destroy. If you have "flown away" go back home. Satan is in his glory because he has again managed to divide and conquer! Take back the ground that he stole from you; he is a thief! "The thief comes only to **steal, and kill, and destroy**; I came that they might have life, and might have it abundantly." John 10:10. Give God the victory and the testimony by turning this around for **His** glory! Instead of throwing away "your cross" (your troubled marriage), pick it up again and follow Him!

Take up his cross daily. "And He was saying to them all, 'If anyone wishes to come after Me, let him deny himself, and **take up his cross daily**, and follow Me.' " Luke 9:23. Be sure that your cross isn't heavier than He has designed for you; take off all your lack of forgiveness and bitterness. It's a heavy weight to carry and, eventually, you won't be able to continue to carry it. You may not even be able to lift it up now, to begin to follow Him.

Take off any "works of the flesh." The flesh will wear you out and break you down. Let go and let God restore. Use this time to fellowship with the Lord! If your cross feels too heavy to bear, there are burdens on your cross that *you* have put there. He does not lie and He has promised that He wouldn't give us more than we could bear!

There is no one besides Thee. Now let us together pray as Asa prayed in 2Chron. 14:11: "Lord, there is no one besides Thee to help in the battle between the powerful and those who have no strength; so help us, O Lord our God, for we trust in Thee, and in Thy name have come against this multitude. O Lord, thou art our God; let not man prevail against Thee."

Don't follow the world's way; trust only in Him. I promise you that He will never let you down. Only as you compromise or look to the flesh for strength and protection will things go awry. Still, it may take going through the fire of endurance (*with* Him) to reach the victory He has waiting for you. Will you pick up your cross and follow Him?

How much faith do you have? Do you have the faith to step out and allow the Lord to fight for you without a lawyer? Please pray for the strength to put all your trust in Jesus – He won't let you down!

Personal commitment: to trust God alone. "Based on what I have learned in Scripture, I commit to trusting the Lord to fight for me in this battle. I will release my attorney (if I have one) and I will not show up in court (unless I will be in contempt)."

Date: _____ Signed:_____

——————— Chapter 14———————

Who is Without Sin?

Adultery
Grounds for Forgiveness

Note: This chapter is designed to minister to men whose wives are in adultery. If it is **you** who has committed adultery, please do not use this chapter to judge your wife's lack of forgiveness towards you!

Should adultery ever be forgiven? What did Jesus do? This is what He said to the woman caught in adultery: "Did no one condemn you? …Neither do I condemn you; go your way. From now on, sin no more." John 8:10-11.

Are you without sin, that you should cast the first stone at your wife? Jesus also said, to the people who wanted this woman found in adultery punished, "He who is without sin among you, cast the first stone." John 8:7. Are you without sin? "If we say that we have no sin, we are deceiving ourselves, and the truth is not in us." 1John 1:8.

If you choose not to forgive her. What are the grave consequences of not forgiving? "But if you do not forgive men for their transgressions, your heavenly Father will not forgive your transgressions." Matt. 6:15.

When God refers to adulterers and fornicators, He says, "And such *were* some of you; but you were washed, but you were **sanctified**, but you were justified in the name of the Lord Jesus Christ and in the spirit of our God." 1Cor. 6:9-11. "For…the unbelieving wife is sanctified through her believing husband; for otherwise your children are unclean, but now they are holy." 1Cor. 7:14. Since you and your wife are one flesh, we, at Restore Ministries, suggest that you draw closer to God and allow Him to begin transforming you into His image. As you cleave to God, wonderful and amazing things will begin happening to your wife since you are one flesh!

But this is not the first time she has committed adultery! Let us remember what Jesus said to us when asked how often we are to forgive someone. "If he sins against you seven times a day, and returns to you seven times, saying 'I repent,' forgive him." Luke 17:4.

But she hasn't repented! As Jesus hung on the cross for *your* sins, He cried out, "Father forgive them, for they know not what they do." Luke 23:34. Will you demand from your wife what Jesus, though completely innocent, did not demand from those persecuting him?

"Don't be overcome with evil, but overcome evil with good." God specifically asked His prophet Hosea to remarry his wife, Gomer, even after she was blatantly unfaithful to him. "...for she is not my wife, and I am not her husband...." "...then she will say, 'I will go back to my first husband, for it was better for me then than now.' " "Then the Lord said to me (Hosea), 'Go again, love a woman who is loved by her husband, yet an adulteress...' " Hosea 2:2, 2:7, 3:1 God used the story of Hosea and Gomer to show His commitment to His own bride, the Church.

Was lost. "And the older son said to his father 'But when this son of yours came, who devoured your wealth with harlots, you killed the fatted calf for him.' " Luke 15:30. The father responded to his older son, "But we had to be merry and rejoice, for this brother of yours was dead and has begun to live, and **was lost** and has been found." Luke 15:32.

Can I ever trust her again? God said to trust <u>Him</u>, and then you will be blessed with a faithful wife. "...Cursed is the man who trusts mankind and makes flesh his strength… Blessed is the man who trusts in the Lord and whose trust **is** the Lord." Jer.17:5,7.

How can I help my wife? Help your wife by forgiving her, by loving her, and by praying for her. "Keep watching and praying, that you may not come into temptation; the spirit is willing, but the flesh is weak." Mark 14:38. Every one who **allowed** God to turn the heart of their spouse testifies that God removed their spouses yearning for another. God may bring other tests into our lives to be sure, but not adultery. When God heals, it is finished. It is a complete healing and deliverance from adultery. But, remember, if you sow in the flesh, you will reap in the flesh. Men, if you coerce or entice your wife to return home, you will reap consequences. Learn to wait. When it is the blessing of the Lord, He will add no sorrow to it! (Prov. 10:22)

What does His Word say we are to do (or not do) if our wife is in adultery?

We are not to flatter. We are, instead, to edify. "A man who flatters his neighbor is spreading a net for his steps." Prov. 29:5. "Let no unwholesome word proceed out of your mouth, but only such a word as is good for edification." Eph. 4:29. While you are busy tearing your wife down and trying to hurt her, the OM is building her up. While you were disagreeing with your wife, the OM was agreeing with her. You MUST edify your wife.

What, you may ask, is the difference between flattering and edifying? When someone flatters, their purpose or motivation is to gain some benefit from their statement(s). One who has chosen to edify, or build up another, is giving from their heart and expecting nothing in return. Two men can be saying the same thing, yet their motives can be very different.

God may bring on His wrath, *if* YOU walk in humility. "Therefore consider the members of your earthly body as dead to immorality, impurity, passion, evil desire, and greed, which amounts to idolatry. For on account of these things the wrath of God will come." Col. 3:5-6. "For we know Him who said,

'Vengeance is mine, I will repay,' and again, 'The Lord will judge His people.' It is a terrifying thing to fall into the hands of the living God." Hebrew 10:30-31.

Again, if you haven't forgiven, you may be joyful about the "wrath from God." This, too, is dangerous. "Do not rejoice when your enemy falls, and do not let your heart be glad when he stumbles; lest the LORD see it and be displeased, And He turn away His anger from him." Prov. 24:18.

Do not be deceived into thinking that you need to look into what your wife is doing. "For nothing is hidden that shall not become evident, nor anything secret that shall not be known and come to light." Luke 8:17. "For it is disgraceful *even to speak* of the things which are done by them in secret." Eph. 5:12. (The testimonies of those who did spy or investigate are **tragic**. Please don't make the same mistake!)

The Adulterer and the Adulteress

She does not know it. "She does not ponder the path of life; her ways are *unstable*, **she does not know it**." Prov. 5:3-6. Do not expect your wife to act logically or listen to reason if she is in adultery. The very worst thing you can do is to try to talk to her about her situation. And the second worst thing is to seem baffled by how she is acting or what she is doing. Helping you understand this tragic situation is why we have put this chapter in the book. This is a spiritual battle, so fight it spiritually by no longer perishing for a lack of knowledge.

The adulteress is out of the home! "A woman comes to meet him, dressed as a harlot and cunning of heart, *she is boisterous and rebellious; her feet do not remain at home*." Prov. 7:5. Please read Lesson 13 "Provide for His Own" in *A Wise Man,* our manual for men. It answers many of the questions you may be asking yourself now like: Could my wife's "career" outside the home have been part of the cause of our home crumbling? Why did I allow or encourage my wife to help me provide? Now she has her own money, her own friends, and her own life! "But if anyone does not provide for his own, and especially for those of his household, he has denied the faith, and is worse than an unbeliever." 1Tim. 5:8. You must claim His promise: "And my God shall supply all your needs according to His riches in glory in Christ Jesus." Phil. 4:19.

The adulteress is deceived into thinking that she has done nothing wrong. "This is the way of an adulterous woman: she eats and wipes her mouth, and says, *'I have done nothing wrong.'* " Prov. 30:20. If you desire your wife to return to you, follow these guidelines. "Or do you think lightly of the riches of His kindness and forbearance and patience, not knowing that the **kindness** of God *leads you to repentance?*" Rom. 2:4. Show your wife kindness, not condemnation or criticism. Make sure that she KNOWS that you take the full responsibility for her adultery, just as Jesus takes the full responsibility for our sins. Then nail her sins to the cross of Jesus and walk in the love and forgiveness that will **annihilate** the enemy and his schemes!

This is a Spiritual battle. It must be fought and won in the Spirit. Please reread Chapter 15 "Weapons of Our Warfare" to understand more about Spiritual Warfare. We also have examples of prayers in Chapter 17 that work mightily against adultery. Always ignore and resist the temptation to fight in the flesh, either viciously or enticingly. Books, talk shows, and well-meaning friends may try to sway you to either administer the "tough-love" approach, which will lead to even more hurt and a complete disaster of your restoration, or to be more romantic or seductive to win her back. Neither of these is the cause nor the solution to this sin. **It is a Spiritual Battle**. It must be fought and **won** *in the Spirit.* Love, as described in 1Corinthians chapter 13, is always the right response!

Once your wife shows you that she feels she is able to trust you (because she knows that you are not going to try to make her to come back, but that you have let her go) then it is time to allure her as it describes in the book of Hosea. If you want a good teaching on this topic, the Q&A video "Alluring and Unconditional Love" has helped many who are now restored.

By agreement. Many ask what they should do if their unfaithful wives approach them for physical intimacy. "But because of immoralities, let each man have his own wife, and let each woman have her own husband. Let the husband fulfill his duty to his wife, and likewise also the wife to her husband. The wife does not have authority over her own body, but the husband does; and likewise also the husband does not have authority over his own body, but the wife does. Stop depriving one another, *except* **by agreement** *for a time that you may devote yourselves to prayer*, and come together again lest Satan tempt you because of your lack of self- control." 1Cor. 7:2-5.

This verse clearly covers those who are still legally married. If a divorce has taken place, give no appearance of evil. This is the time that you must abstain from intimacy even if she pursues you.

Personal Commitment: To forgive. "Based on what I have learned in Scripture, I commit to trusting the Lord and refuse to fight in the flesh. I will continue to forgive my wife daily and forgive all others who have been or are currently involved. I will stay meek as I walk in a spirit of forgiveness."

Date: _____ Signed:_____

Chapter 15

He Gives Us the Keys

"I will give you the keys
of the kingdom of heaven."
Matt. 16:19.

Jesus gave us the keys of heaven to "bind up" the evil and "loose" the good. "I will give you the keys of the kingdom of heaven; and whatever you shall bind on earth shall be bound in heaven, and whatever you shall loose on earth shall be loosed in heaven." Matt. 16:19.

Remove the evil. Find a verse concerning what you want to remove. When someone is "bound" in sin, you must first bind that "strong man," which is what has a hold of the person you are praying for. Search for the verse that you can pray. Here is the principle, "But *no one* can enter the strong man's house...unless he *first* **binds the strong man**...." Mark 3:27.

Replace the evil with good. This is very important! "When the unclean spirit goes out of a man, it passes through waterless places seeking rest, and not finding any, it says, '*I will return to my house from which I came.*' And when it comes, it finds it swept and put in order. Then it goes and takes along seven other spirits more evil than itself, and they go in and live there; and the last state of that man becomes **worse than the first**." Luke 11:24-26.

If you fail to replace. If you fail to replace what you have removed, it will become worse than before you prayed. You must always replace something evil with something good. This is one reason why so many who go on diets actually get fatter. They stop eating all the things that are not healthy for them but they never replace the bad food with something good, like prayer, going for a walk, exercising, or eating something else that *is* good for them.

Replace the lies with the truth. The truth is found in His Word. Pray a verse of blessing over your wife, such as something from Proverbs 31. Remember, unless what you hear, what you read, what someone tells you matches up with a principle in God's Word, IT IS A LIE!

Replace the "arm of the flesh" with the "Lord." Replace trusting in "the arm of the flesh" (you, a friend, whoever) with trusting in God. "Finally, be strong in the Lord, and in the strength of His might." Eph. 6:10.

Replace running away with running to Him! "God is our refuge and our strength, a very present help in time of trouble." Ps. 46:1. Run to the book of Psalms!

As a member of our Restoration Fellowship, you could go to our Daily Devotional on our website. Go to www.RestoreMinistries.net to join!

Replace crying out to another with crying out to Him! He promises to hear you and to lift you up immediately! But you **must** cry out! "**Ask** *and it shall be given* you; seek and you shall find." Matt. 7:7.

Preparing for War

Put on your armor daily as described in Ephesians 6:10-18.

The schemes of the devil. "Finally, be strong in the Lord and in the strength of His might. Put on the full armor of God, that you may be able to stand firm against the schemes of the devil." Eph. 6:10-11. Remember who the real enemy is: satan, not your wife.

The full armor of God. "For our struggle is not against flesh and blood, but against the rulers, against the powers, against the world forces of this darkness, against the spiritual forces of wickedness in the heavenly places. Therefore, take up the full armor of God, that you may be able to resist in the evil day." Eph. 6:12-13. You must resist the **fear** that causes you to want to run away or give up; stand firm and, having done everything, continue to stand firm. Psalm 37 is good to pray if you are plagued with fear.

Stand firm. "Stand firm therefore, having girded your loins with truth…." Eph. 6:14. People talk about "stepping out in faith." At certain times it may be best to stop moving and just stand firm! It may be the difference between trusting and tempting God. Sometimes we feel like we are taking a "step of faith," but we are actually throwing ourselves off a cliff. Yet, as you will see later in this lesson, sometimes we are asked to step out and walk on water, as Peter was asked to do. Discernment is needed here. *The amount of urgency you are feeling at a particular time may help you to determine the will of the Lord. Our "flesh" usually brings about urgency; God usually says to wait.*

His righteousness. "…and having put on the breastplate of righteousness…." Eph. 6:14. God is talking about His righteousness, not yours. He tells us in His Word that our righteousness is nothing but "filthy rags" (Isa. 64:6).

Walk in peace. "And having shod your feet with the preparation of the gospel of peace…" Eph. 6:15. You can claim the promise in Matthew: "Blessed are the peacemakers!" Be peaceful with EVERYONE at ALL times!

The shield of faith. "In addition to all, taking up the shield of faith with which you will be able to ***extinguish all the flaming missiles*** of the evil one." Eph. 6:16. You must have faith – not in yourself or someone else like a judge – faith in God, in Him alone! Circumstance has nothing to do with faith. Believe His Word alone for the truth about your situation.

Helmet of salvation. "And take the helmet of salvation." Eph. 6:17. You must be saved; you must be one of His children to really win a difficult spiritual battle. It's as easy as talking to God right now. Just tell Him in your own words that you need Him, now. Ask Him to make Himself real to you. Ask Him to forgive you for your sins and give Him your life, a life that is messed up, and ask the Lord to make it new.

Tell Him that you will do whatever He asks, since He is now your Lord. Ask Him to "save you" from your situation and from the eternity that is waiting for all those who do not accept His gift of eternal life. Thank Him for His death on the cross, the death that He died for you. You can now trust that you will no longer live alone; God will always be with you and you will spend eternity in Heaven!

Sword of the Spirit. "Take...the sword of the Spirit which is the word of God." Eph. 6:17. This is exactly what we have been teaching: use His Word to win the battle. When the battle is the Lord's, the victory is ours! Write down on 3x5 cards the Scriptures you need to help in this war for your marriage and family. Keep them with you at all times in your purse. When you feel an attack coming on, like fear, read the verses that pertain to fear. (See Rom. 8:15 and Psalm 23 for wonderful verses to attack fear.) Cry out to God. Stand firm in faith. "Be still and know that I am God." Ps. 46:10.

Pray at all times. "With all prayer and petition pray at all times in the Spirit." Eph. 6:18. Pray from deep in your Spirit. Have designated times of prayer three times a day (as Daniel did). That was one of the reasons he was thrown into the lions' den. Don't worry, but remember that even if you are in essence thrown into the lions' den, God will shut all the lions' mouths!

Be on the alert. "And with this in view, be on the alert with all perseverance and petition for all the saints." Eph. 6:18. Pray for another person you know each time you feel overwhelmed. "Most gladly therefore, I will rather boast about my weaknesses, that the power of Christ may dwell in me. Therefore I am well content with weaknesses, with insults, with distresses, with persecutions, with difficulties, for Christ's sake; for when I am weak, then I am strong." Phil 12:9-10.

Pray for those who persecute you. God also asked that we pray for someone else: our enemies, every one of them. Pray for them and ask God to show you what He wants you to do to bless them. It wasn't until after Job prayed for his so-called friends that God restored what Job had lost. "And the Lord restored the fortunes of Job when he prayed for his friends, and the Lord increased all that Job had twofold." Job 42:10. "But I say to you, love your enemies, and pray for those who persecute you." He goes on to tell you why: "in order that you may be sons of your Father who is in heaven." Matt. 5:44-45.

Know God's Word

His Word will not come back void. You must know and learn God's Word. You need to set out to find the blessed promises of God. These principles are from His Word and when we speak His Word to Him by prayer, it will not come back void.

That is His promise to you! "So shall My word be which goes forth from My mouth; *it shall not return to Me void* (empty), without **accomplishing** what I desire and without **succeeding** in the matter for which I sent it." Isaiah 55:11. His desire is that you may overcome the evils in this world.

Search for His principles throughout your Bible. Seek understanding. God says if you seek you will find. God's Word gives wisdom. Looking deeper into the meaning gives you a better understanding. "And I say to you, ask, and it shall be given to you; **seek**, and **you shall find**; knock, and it shall be opened to you." Luke 11:9. And once you know what to do, then you can apply it to your life. "By **wisdom** a house is *built*, and by **understanding** it is *established*; and by **knowledge** the *rooms are filled* with all *precious* and *pleasant riches.*" Prov. 24:3-4.

Read His Word with delight. Mark the verses in your Bible. "Delight yourself in the Lord; and He will give you the desires of your heart." Ps. 37:4. Take the time to mark verses for quick reference in times of distress (or when leading another to the truth). In Luke 4:4-10 what did Jesus answer when Satan was trying to tempt Him? "And Jesus answered him, 'It is written…, It is written…, for it is written….'"

Memorize. Meditate day and night. Memorize the promises you find so that the blessed assurance of them may sink into your soul. You must learn and know God's promises if you ever want to depend on Him alone. "But his delight is in the law of the Lord, And in His law he **meditates day and night**. And he will be like a tree firmly planted by streams of water, which yields its fruit in its season, And its leaf does not wither; And in whatever he does, he prospers." Ps. 1:2.

No matter how bad things may seem; God is in control. Our comfort is found in knowing that God is in control, not us and certainly not Satan. "Simon, Simon, behold, Satan has **demanded** *permission* to sift you like wheat; but I have prayed for you, that your faith may not fail; and you, when *once you have turned again*, strengthen your brothers." Luke 22:31-32.

Sifting. Jesus knew the outcome, yet Peter still had to go through the "sifting" to be ready for God's calling on his life. Will you be ready when He calls you? "And let endurance have its perfect result, that you may be **perfect and complete**, *lacking in nothing*." Jas. 1:4.

Spiritual Warfare

Take your thoughts captive. Your battle WILL be won or lost in your mind. "We are **destroying speculations** and every lofty thing raised up against the knowledge of God, and we are **taking every thought captive** to the obedience of Christ, and we are ready to punish all disobedience, whenever your obedience is complete." 2Cor. 10:5-6. Don't play into the enemies' hands. Don't entertain evil thoughts. Take them captive!

The Power of Three

Two or three gathered together. Find two other MEN who will pray with you. "But Moses' hands were heavy. Then they took a stone and put it under him, and he sat on it; and Aaron and Hur supported his hands, one on one side and one on the other. Thus his hands were steady until the sunset…when Moses held his hand up, then Israel prevailed, and when he let his hand down Amalek (the enemy) prevailed." Ex. 17:11-12.

Find **two** other **men** to hold you up so you won't become too weary. Pray and ask God to help you find two others who are like-minded. You can also find an Encouragement Partner on our website.

The power of three. "And if **one** can *overpower him* who is alone, **two** can *resist* him. A cord of **three** strands is not quickly *torn apart*." Eccl. 4:12.

To lift the other up. "**Two** are *better* than **one** because they have a *good return for their labor*. For if either of them *falls*, the *one will lift up his companion*. But woe to the one who falls when there is not another to lift him up." Eccl. 4:9-10.

He is there with you. "For where **two or three** have *gathered* together in My name, there I am in their midst." Matt. 18:20. "Then Nebuchadnezzar the king was astounded and stood up in haste; he responded and said to his high officials, 'Was it not **three men** we cast bound into the midst of the fire?' They answered and said to the king, 'Certainly, O king.' He answered and said, 'Look! I see **four men** loosed and walking about in the midst of the fire without harm, and the appearance of the **fourth** is like a *son of the gods*!' " Dan. 3:24. You are never alone!

Agreement. "Again I say to you, that if **two** of you *agree* on earth about **anything** that they may ask, it shall be done for them by My Father who is in heaven." Matt. 18:19. When you are wrestling with peace about something, call someone who will believe with you and pray in agreement.

Standing in the gap. "And I searched for a man among them who should build up the wall and **stand in the gap** before Me for the land, that I should not destroy it; but I *found no one*." Ezek. 22:30.

Pray for one another. "Therefore, confess your sins to one another, and *pray for one another*, so that you may be healed. The effective prayer of a righteous man can accomplish much." Jas. 5:16. Also, confession to a like-minded man is the best way to obtain a pure heart.

Make your confession. Ezra knew what to do when praying: "Now while Ezra was praying and **making confession**, weeping and prostrating himself before the house of God...." Ezra 10:1. Keep confessing the truth.

When do you give up praying? Never! We have a wonderful example of the fact that God does not always mean "no" when we don't see immediate answers to our prayers.

Your faith is great. The Canaanite woman continued to beg Jesus for her daughter's healing. The result: "...Then Jesus answered and said to her, 'O woman, **your faith is great**; be it done for you as you wish.' And her daughter was healed at once." Matt. 15:2. When we pray for something that is clearly in God's will and it seems to have gone unheard or He has said what we think is "No," God may simply want us to keep on asking, waiting, pleading, fasting, believing, weeping, laying ourselves prostate before Him!

The battle for his soul. Are you unequally yoked? The real battle in your home is the battle for your wife's soul! Are you unequally yoked? Remember that you have the promise: "...you will be saved, you and all your household." Acts 11:14.

Prayer and Fasting

Prayer AND fasting. Jesus told His apostles, "But this kind does not go out *except* by **prayer and fasting**." Matt. 17:21. If you have been praying fervently and have checked to see if your ways are pure, then fasting may be called for. There are different lengths of fasts:

Three-day fast. Esther fasted "for favor" from her husband the king. She fasted 3 days "for favor." "Go, assemble all the Jews who are found in Susa, and **fast** for me; do not eat or drink for *three days*, night or day. I and my maidens also will **fast** in the same way." Esth. 4:16.

Day fast. The day fast begins in the evening after your evening meal. You drink only water until the 24-hour period is complete, and then eat the next day's evening meal. You fast and pray during this time for your petition. This fast can be done a couple of times a week.

Seven-day fast. "Now it came about when I heard these words, I sat down and wept and mourned **for days**; and **I was fasting and praying** before the God of heaven." Neh. 1:4. Usually it will be during great sorrow that you are "called" to fast for seven days.

My knees are weak from fasting. When you are hungry or weak, use that time for prayer and reading His Word. "**My knees are weak from fasting**; and my flesh has grown lean, without fatness." Ps. 109:24.

In order to be seen. Keep as quiet about your fast as is possible. During the fast, you are to be silent, never complaining or drawing attention to yourself. "And whenever you **fast**, do not put on a **gloomy face** as the *hypocrites* do, for they neglect their appearance **in order to be seen** fasting by men. Truly I say to you, they have their *reward in full*. But you, when you fast, anoint your head, and wash your face so *that you may not be seen fasting by men*, but by your Father who is in secret; and *your Father who sees in secret will repay you*." Matt. 6:16-18.

Many write to us and say they can't fast. If it is for medical reasons, then fast "any good thing." If, however, you think you can't fast because you are working – you are selling yourself and God short!

Intensity of your trials is a sign that you are close to victory. Your trials may intensify when you are close to gaining the victory. "For this reason, **rejoice**, O heavens and you who dwell in them. Woe to the earth and the sea, because the devil has come down to you, having great wrath, *knowing* that he has only a **short time**." Rev. 12:12.

No one should boast. When a battle is won or when the war is over, let us only boast in Him. Let us remain humble. "For by grace you have been saved through faith; and that not of yourselves, it is the **gift of God**; not as a result of works, that *no one should boast*." Eph. 2:8-9. We all have sinned and come short of the glory of God. So let us remember this when the battle is won. Our righteousness is nothing but filthy rags. Glory in Him!

Chapter 16

I Searched for a Man

"And I searched for a man among them
who should build up the wall and
stand in the gap before Me
for the land, that I should not destroy it;
but I found no one."
Ezekiel 22:30

"Dear Heavenly Father, I enter into my place of prayer, now that I have shut the door, I pray to you my Father in secret. And as you see me here in secret you will reward me openly. It is written that all things, whatsoever ye shall ask in prayer, believing, ye shall receive.

"O God, thou art my God; early will I seek thee; my soul longs for Thee in a dry and thirsty land, where no water is. Lord, there is no one besides Thee to help in the battle between the powerful and those who have no strength; so help us, O Lord our God, for we trust in Thee, and in Thy name have come against this multitude. O Lord, Thou art my God; let not man prevail against Thee.

"Your eyes, Lord, move to and fro throughout the whole earth that you may strongly support those hearts who are completely Yours. Search my heart.

"For though we walk in the flesh, we do not war after the flesh, for the weapons of our warfare are not carnal, but mighty through God to the pulling down of strongholds. Casting down imaginations, and every high thing that exalts itself against the knowledge of God, and bringing into captivity every thought to the obedience of Christ, and You have readiness to revenge all disobedience when Your obedience is fulfilled.

"O let the evil of the wicked come to an end, but establish the righteous. I shall not be afraid of evil tidings; my heart is fixed, trusting in the Lord. My heart is established; I shall not be afraid, until I see my desire come upon the enemy.

"Whatsoever ye shall bind on earth shall be bound in heaven; and whatsoever ye shall loose on earth shall be loosed in heaven. I ask you, Heavenly Father, to rebuke and to bind Satan in the name and through the blood of my Lord Jesus Christ. Hedge up his way with thorns, and build a wall against him so that he cannot find his paths.

"Abraham hoped against hope, believed in hope, and being not weak in faith, staggered not at the promise of God through unbelief; but was strong in faith, giving glory to God. He was fully persuaded that what He had promised, He was able to perform.

"For we are saved by hope; but hope that is seen is not hope; for what man seeth, why doth he yet hope for it? But if we hope for what we see not, then do we with patience wait for it. I had fainted, unless I had believed to see the goodness of the Lord in the land of the living. Wait on the Lord; be of good courage and He will strengthen thine heart, yes, wait on the Lord. But they that wait upon the Lord shall renew their strength; they shall mount up with wings as eagles; they shall run and not be weary; and they shall walk and not faint.

"For since the beginning of the world men have not heard, nor perceived by the ear, neither hath the eye seen, O God, beside thee, what He hath prepared for him who waiteth for Him. Surely goodness and mercy shall follow me all the days of my life and I will dwell in the house of the Lord forever. Amen."

Prayer for Those in Adultery

"I ask you, Father, to rebuke and bind Satan in the Name and through the Blood of the Lord Jesus Christ. I ask you to build a Hedge of Thorns around my wife so that anyone who is interested in her will lose interest and leave. I base my prayer on the command of Your Word, which says, 'What therefore God has joined together, let no man separate.' I thank you, Father, for hearing and answering my prayer. Amen."

"Therefore I will hedge up her way with thorns, and I will build a wall against her so that she cannot find her paths. And she will pursue her lovers, but will not overtake them; and she will seek them, but will not find them. Then she will say, 'I will go back to my husband. For it was better for me then than now!' Therefore I will allure her, bring her into the wilderness, and speak kindly to her. For I will remove the names of Baals from her mouth. Then the Lord said to me, 'Go again, love a woman yet an adulterer.' " *From Hosea 6.*

"Drink water from your own cistern, and fresh water from your own well. Should your springs be dispersed abroad, streams of water in the streets? Let them be yours alone, and not for strangers with you. Let your fountains be blessed, and rejoice in the wife of your youth. As a loving hind and graceful doe, let her breasts satisfy you at all times. For why should you, my son, be exhilarated with an adulteress, and embrace the bosom of a foreigner? Can man take fire to his bosom, and his clothes not be burned? Or can a man walk on hot coals, and his feet not be scorched? So is one who goes in to his neighbor's wife. Whoever touches her will not go unpunished. For the ways of a man are before the eyes of the Lord, and He watches all his paths." *From Proverbs 5.*

"For though we walk in the flesh, we do not war according to the flesh, for the weapons of our warfare are not of the flesh, but divinely powerful for the destruction of fortresses. We are destroying every lofty thing raised up against the knowledge of God, and we are taking every thought captive to the obedience of Christ.

"For I now rejoice, not that you were made sorrowful, but that you were made sorrowful to the point of repentance; for you were made sorrowful according to the will of God, in order that you might not suffer loss in anything through us. For the sorrow that is according to the will of God produces a repentance without regret, leading to salvation; but the sorrow of the world produces death." *Taken from 2Cor. 10.*

"God gave us a ministry of reconciliation, namely, that God Himself was in Christ reconciling the world to Himself, not counting their trespasses against them, and He has committed to us the word of reconciliation. Therefore, we are ambassadors for Christ, as though God were entreating through us; we beg you on behalf of Christ, be reconciled to God." *Taken from 2Cor. 5.*

"There will be more joy in heaven over one sinner who repents, than over ninety-nine righteous persons who do not need repentance. Yes, there is joy in the presence of the angels of God over one sinner who repents. For Jesus said, 'He who is without sin among you, let him be the first to throw a stone. I do not condemn you; go your way. From now on sin no more.'" *Taken from Luke 15.*

"Neither do I condemn you." *John 8.*

Prayer to Restore

"Hear my prayer, O Lord, give ear to my cry, do not be silent at my tears. Put my tears in a bottle, are they not in Thy book? Since I am afflicted and needy, let the Lord be mindful of me. Thou art my help and my deliverer. Do not delay, O my God." *From Psalms 56 and 40.*

"Though they intend evil against Thee, and devise a plot, they will not succeed. When my enemies turn back they stumble and perish before Thee. Thou hast blotted out their name forever and ever. The very memory of them has perished. Yet a little while and the wicked man will be no more. And you will look carefully for his place and he will not be there. But the humble will inherit the land and will delight themselves in abundant prosperity." *From Psalm 21.*

"Thou dost surround the righteous with a shield. In peace I will both lie down and sleep. For Thou alone dost make me dwell in safety. Offer to God a sacrifice of thanksgiving, and call upon Me in the day of trouble. I shall rescue you, and you will honor Me." *From Psalm 4.*

"Be strong, and let your heart take courage, all you who hope in the Lord. Be their shepherd also and carry them forever. I would have despaired if I had not believed that I would see the goodness of the Lord, in the land of the living. Wait for the Lord; be strong and let your heart take courage. Yes, wait for the Lord." *From Psalm 27.*

May God Grant You Victory!

Personal commitment: to battle in the Spirit for my wife and my marriage. "Based on what I have learned from God's Word, I commit to battling in the Spirit rather than continuing to battle in the flesh. I recognize that when I battle in the flesh I am losing the spiritual battle. Therefore I commit to spending my energy, time and thought life in the spiritual battle for my marriage and family."

Date: _____ Signed:_____

Chapter 17

Opening the Windows of Heaven

"Test Me now in this," says the Lord of hosts,
"if I will not open for you the windows of heaven,
and pour out for you a blessing until it overflows."
Malachi 3:10

This is a pretty powerful statement from God. Nowhere else in Scripture does God tell us to test Him, except here in this verse. What is it that God says will cause Him to open the windows of heaven, pouring out His blessing on us until it overflows?

"'Bring the whole tithe into the storehouse, so that there may be food in My house, and test Me now in this,' says the Lord of hosts, 'if I will not open for you the windows of heaven, and pour out for you a blessing until it overflows'" (Mal. 3:10).

Did you see it? It's tithing. Tithing will cause God to open the windows of heaven and shower His blessings over your life!

Many Christians shy away from learning as much as they can about this important principle, but please don't miss this! God wants us to be faithful and obedient in **all** things, and when we neglect or choose to be disobedient in one area of our lives, it spills over into other areas as well.

What exactly is tithing? It is giving back to God ten percent of the first of your increase.

Our society as a whole is ignorant of this principle. Many churches fail their people by neglecting to teach the importance of tithing. Why is it so serious? Because God is angry when we fail to give back to Him what is rightfully His. "The earth is the Lord's, and all it contains, the world, and those who dwell in it" (Ps. 24:1). Tithing is an act of worship.

There are too many Christians who either live in poverty or are in as much debt as the unbeliever. But God wants to make every believer "the head and not the tail." He wants you to be "above" and "not be underneath" debt or anything else that will rule or control your life (Deut. 28:13). We are told, "Owe nothing to anyone except to love one another . . ." (Rom. 13:8). "The rich rules over the poor, and the borrower becomes the lender's slave" (Prov. 22:7).

Most Christians in the United States are blessed with so much, especially if we look at other nations and the level of poverty at which most people of the world live. We spend our earnings on pleasures while our churches, missionaries, and ministries struggle to make ends meet. Why? Because we try to hold onto what is not rightfully ours to keep.

We take but give little. "Now this I say, he who **sows sparingly** shall also **reap sparingly;** and he who **sows bountifully** shall also **reap bountifully.** Let each one do just as he has purposed in his heart, not grudgingly or under compulsion, for God loves a cheerful giver" (2 Cor. 9:6).

We ask and wonder why we don't receive. "You ask and do not receive, because you ask with wrong motives, so that you may **spend it on your pleasures**" (James 4:3).

God wanted to **bless** His people, but He did not because they were unwilling to give into His storehouse. He tells them in Hag. 1:6–7, "'You have sown much, but harvest little; you eat, but there is not enough to be satisfied; you drink, but there is not enough to become drunk; you put on clothing, but no one is warm enough; and he who earns, earns wages to put into a purse with holes. Thus says the Lord of hosts, 'Consider your ways!'"

"'You look for much, but behold, it comes to little; when you bring it home, **I blow it away.** Why?' declares the Lord of hosts, 'Because of My house which lies desolate, while each of you runs to his own house'" (Hag. 1:9).

Understanding Tithing

It is ironic that so many Christians erroneously believe that they are not able to "afford" to tithe and bless God through offerings. The truth is that they are simply caught in a vicious cycle that only obedience and faith can cure. They can't afford to give because they rob God to pay men, thereby robbing themselves of being blessed!

As a matter of fact, it is when we are in deep poverty that God asks us to give. The Christians in Macedonia understood and applied this principle of giving: "Out of the most severe trial, their overflowing joy and their extreme poverty welled up in rich generosity" (2 Cor. 8:2). Sounds a bit like many of us, doesn't it?

Why 10%?

The word tithe in the Hebrew is **"ma'asrah,"** which translates to "a tenth." So whenever God speaks to us in His Word and says to "tithe," He is saying to give Him a tenth.

Why should I give my tithe *first,* before paying my bills?

This is the principle of "first fruits" of our labor. Deuteronomy 18:4 tells us, "You shall give him the **first fruits** of your grain, your new wine, and your oil, and the first shearing of your sheep." Then, in Exodus 34:24 and 26, God says, "For I will drive out nations before you and enlarge your borders. . . . You shall bring the **very first** of the **first fruits** of your soil into the house of the Lord your God. . . ."

This also is confirmed in the New Testament when Jesus tells us in Matthew 6:33, "But seek **first** His kingdom and His righteousness; and **all** these things shall be added to you."

Where should I tithe?

Malachi 3:10 tells us, "'Bring the whole tithe into the **storehouse**, so that there may be food in My house, and test Me now in this,' says the Lord of hosts, 'if I will not open for you the windows of heaven, and pour out for you a blessing until it overflows.'"

Your **storehouse** is where you are spiritually fed. Many Christians make the mistake of giving where they are
not spiritually fed but would rather give where they see there is a need—but this is foolishness. It is like going to a restaurant, ordering a meal, but when the check comes telling the cashier that you would rather give to the restaurant down the street that is not doing too well!

If you are attending a church where you are being spiritually fed, then you should be tithing at least a tenth of your income to your home church. That means that if you attend church and feel led to sow financially into our ministry (or any other ministry or missions), then this would be an offering "above and beyond" your tithe. We don't want you to steal from your church to sow into our ministry "for this would be unprofitable for you" (Heb. 15:17).

However, many of our fellowship members who are **not** attending a church (for a variety of reasons) *and* are being fed through our ministry tithe by sowing into restoring marriages, since this is where they are being spiritually fed.

Again, as we have encouraged you throughout this book—seek **God.** This goes for everything, including your finances. Then be obedient and faithful to **Him!**

Don't make the mistake of diligently following all the principles for restoring your marriage yet fail to tithe, lest you find your marriage unrestored because you are stealing from God.

Remember, Malachi 3:8–10 tells us, **"Will a man rob God?** Yet you are robbing Me! But you say, 'How have we robbed Thee?' In **tithes** *and* **offerings.** You are cursed with a curse, for you are robbing Me, the whole nation of you!"

But since I am not under the law and I live by grace, 10% is no longer required, is it?

God's grace warrants giving more, not less. When we have experienced His forgiveness, His mercy, His compassion, and His sacrifice of His shed blood whereby we become partakers of His glory, it will increase our willingness to give more, certainly not less.

". . . Freely you received, **freely give"** (Matt. 10:8).

"He who did not spare His own Son, but delivered Him over for us all, how will He not also with Him **freely give** us all things?" (Rom. 8:32).

However, ". . . he who *sows* **bountifully** shall also *reap* **bountifully.** Let each one do just as he has purposed in his heart, not grudgingly or under compulsion, for God loves a cheerful giver" (2 Cor. 9:6).

But if we are doubleminded and don't really trust that God will provide for us, "let this man expect that he will receive nothing from the Lord." When we hold onto what we have to try to take care of ourselves, we will never see God's awesome power on our behalf.

God's desire is to pour His power and His blessings into our lives. When we tithe, we are being obedient. But when, out of utter gratitude and worship, we freely give offerings beyond what is commanded, we are truly opening the door for God to pour out His blessings and do His pleasure in our lives.

We know He "is able to do exceedingly and abundantly above all that we ask or think, according to the power that worketh in us" (Eph. 3:20, KJV).

"Seek ye first the kingdom of God and His righteousness, and all these things shall be added unto you" (Matt. 6:33, KJV). Do we take God at His Word or not?

Principles of Stewardship

As we have seen, tithing is an important principle in the Bible. God expects us to tithe back to Him a portion of what He has so generously given to us. Indeed, all that He has given us is still His— we are stewards that He has entrusted to care for the earth and all that is in it. How we handle what He has entrusted to us—our money, our talents, our time and our family—demonstrates our obedience to His Word, our trust in His promise to provide, and, most importantly, our faith in Him.

The way you view and handle your finances is basic to your Christian growth, and understanding God's principles of stewardship will enable you to mature in your spiritual walk and inherit the blessings God has for your life.

As you have read thus far in this book, God deals with many areas in our life that indirectly affect our marriage. It is not enough to concentrate on marriage principles exclusively, but again God is using this trial in your marriage to transform you more into His image as He draws you out of the world's destruction and shows you the pathway to life.

The riches of God are not in order for us to "get rich" in the way the world seeks riches, but instead His blessings are part of our heritage. God wants to prosper us (Jer. 29:11) as long as He knows that we will use our inheritance wisely, without allowing prosperity to bring us to ruin. Giving a car to a child who is too young will most certainly end in tragedy. It is not until a parent sees maturity is he willing to turn over the keys of the car.

God wants us to have a mature attitude toward money, for it has the power to affect our ability to make wise decisions: "Two things I asked of You, do not refuse me before I die: keep deception and lies far from me, give me neither poverty nor riches; feed me with the food that is my portion, that I not be full and deny You and say, 'Who is the Lord?' Or that I not be in want and steal, and profane the name of my God" (Prov. 30:7– 9).

It is clear, though, that it is God's desire to bless His children. Here are more verses that show God's heart toward you as one of His:

"It is the **blessing of the Lord** that **makes rich**, and He adds no sorrow to it" (Prov. 10:22).

"The *reward of humility* and the *fear of the Lord* are riches, honor and life" (Prov. 22:4).

"And by **knowledge** the rooms are filled with all precious and pleasant **riches**" (Prov. 24:4).

"A *faithful man* will *abound* with **blessings**, but he who *makes haste to be rich* will not go unpunished" (Prov. 28:20).

These verses maintain that there are conditions to financial blessings (spiritual maturity) and that this is truly a heart issue (an absence of greed).

All of us want God's blessings upon our life, but did you know that how you handle your financial blessings has a great deal to do with how you grow in the Lord and to what degree God is able to work in your life?

"No one can serve two masters; for either he will hate the one and love the other, or he will stand by and be devoted to the one and despise and be against the other. You cannot serve God and mammon (deceitful riches, money, possessions, or whatever is trusted in)" (Matt. 6:24, AMP).

"Whoever can be trusted with very little can also be trusted with much, and whoever is dishonest with very little will also be dishonest with much. So if you have not been trustworthy in handling worldly wealth, who will trust you with true riches?" (Luke 16:10–11).

To grow in our ability to be used of God, which is spiritual wealth, and gain the *greater* things (having the power and presence of God in our lives) depends in part on how we handle our finances.

To prove this further, there are roughly 500 references in the Bible to faith and 500 to prayer, but there are over 2,000 verses that refer to our finances! In addition to the spiritual laws that were set in place when God created the universe (see chapter 1), God has also established financial laws, which He has shared with us in His Word. We benefit from following the laws or suffer the consequences if we don't. It doesn't matter if we are ignorant of them or have chosen to reject them; these laws, like gravity, exist and cannot be debated.

Principle #1: We reap what we sow.

One of the most important principles of stewardship is sowing and reaping. To reap a harvest, we must sow seed first. There are many Scriptures that give us insight into of the subject of sowing and reaping. Here a just a few:

"Now this I say, he who **sows sparingly** shall also **reap sparingly;** and he who **sows bountifully** shall also
reap bountifully" (2 Cor 9:6).

"Those who sow in tears shall reap with joyful shouting" (Ps. 126:5).

"Do not be deceived, God is not mocked; for whatever a man **sows,** this he will also **reap**" (Gal. 6:7).

"For the one who **sows to his own flesh** shall from the flesh **reap corruption,** but the one who **sows to the Spirit** shall from the Spirit **reap eternal life"** (Gal. 6:8).

"And let us not lose heart in **doing good,** for in due time we **shall reap** if we do **not grow weary"** (Gal. 6:9).

When we sow with the understanding of this principle and with faith in the Lord and His Word, we should **expect** to reap a harvest in and where we have sown! This is really exciting!

No farmer would take the time or the money to sow seed if he did **not** expect to **reap** a harvest. In addition, if he wanted to **reap** a harvest of corn, he would **sow** corn. If he wanted to **reap** wheat, he would **sow** wheat.

Therefore, if you want to reap kindness, sow kindness. If you want to reap forgiveness, forgive! If you want to reap restoration in your marriage, then **sow** into **restoration** by ministering and/or sow financially—then **anticipate** a harvest, since God's principles and His promises are true and He is faithful!!

We can also believe God's promise that sowing into His work means we are investing in our eternal future. "Do not store up for yourselves treasures on earth, where moth and rust destroy, and where thieves break in and steal. But store up for yourselves **treasures in heaven,** where neither moth nor rust destroys, and where thieves do not break in or steal; where your treasure is, there your heart will be also" (Matt. 6:19–21). More importantly, what we do with money here on earth is a true indicator of where our hearts are.

"Now He who supplies seed to the sower and bread for food will supply and multiply your seed **for sowing** and increase the harvest of your righteousness; you will be enriched in everything for all liberality, which through us is producing thanksgiving to God" (2 Cor. 9:10–11).

In other words, when God gives us a bountiful harvest, it is not so we can keep it selfishly for ourselves but so we can sow even more into the kingdom of heaven.

The very wealthy Christians of today are the channels that keep ministries going, send missionaries to foreign lands, and keep our churches flourishing so that they can reach the lost for the Lord. They do not use their finances for their own pleasures but have found that in sowing into the things of God they have true joy and contentment.

However, we must also remember that poverty and prosperity are relative terms. What we call the "poverty level" in the United States would seem like affluence to those in many other countries.

As Christians, we must find contentment in any and every situation. The apostle Paul reminds us in Philippians 4:12: "I know how to get along with **humble means,** and I also know how to live in **prosperity**; in any and every circumstance I have learned the **secret** of being filled and going hungry, both of having **abundance** and suffering **need.**"

Indeed, there are times when God calls His saints to suffering, martyrdom, or poverty (like the poor widow who gave two coins— all she owned) in order to glorify Himself. When He calls us to poverty or suffering, though, He gives us the grace to bear it with joy and thanksgiving—without grumbling or complaining.

While we can't understand all of God's reasons for allowing poverty, we can trust that His ways are higher than our ways. "Out of the most severe trial, their overflowing joy and their **extreme poverty** welled up in **rich generosity.** For I testify that they gave as much as they were able, and even beyond their ability" (2 Cor. 2:8). Sometimes those who suffer the greatest need become the most generous! And for someone with a love of money, a loss of riches may be one of the ways God breaks us, draws us to Himself, and teaches us to rely solely on Him.

However, in our country, poverty and debt do not usually draw the interest or attention of your family, friends, and neighbors. If we have been blessed with much, we must witness to others not by self-righteously preaching to them or condemning their lifestyle but by allowing them to "read" **God** in our lives! "You are our letter, written in our hearts, known and read by all men . . ." (2 Cor. 3:2). We must exhibit the fruits of who our Father is. We must be at peace in the midst of troubles, bless our enemies, freely forgive, and walk in whatever prosperity the Lord allows. Our generosity should glorify

Him and may be the very kindness that God uses to draw others to Himself!

". . . And let them say continually, 'The **Lord** be magnified, **who delights in the prosperity of His servant"**
(Ps. 35:27).

Principle #2: God owns everything.

Psalm 24:1 (NIV) says simply, "The earth is the Lord's, and **everything in it** . . ." Everything we have belongs to God.

"Yours, O Lord, is the greatness and the power and the glory and the majesty and the splendor, for
everything in heaven and earth is **Yours"** (1 Chron. 29:11).

"'The silver is **Mine** and the gold is **Mine**,' declares the Lord Almighty" (Hag. 2:8).

All we have, whether much or little, is on loan to us—we are stewards. Again, it is how we handle what has been entrusted to us (as explained in the Luke 16 parable) that will determine whether He blesses us with more or if He takes away what we already have.

Principle #3: God provides everything.

"Otherwise, you may say in your heart, 'My power and the strength of my hand made me this wealth.' But you shall remember the Lord your God, **for it is He who** *is giving you power* **to make** *wealth,* that He may confirm His covenant which He swore to your fathers, as it is this day. It shall come about if you ever forget the Lord your God and go after other gods and serve them and worship them, I testify against you today that you will surely perish" (Deut. 8:17–19).

"But who am I and who are my people that we should be able to offer as generously as this? For **all things** come from **You**, and from **Your** hand *we have given* You. For we are sojourners before You, and tenants, as all our fathers were; our days on the earth are like a shadow, and there is no hope. O Lord our God, **all this abundance** that we have provided to build **You** a house for Your holy name, **it is from *Your* hand,** and **all is *Yours*** (1 Chron. 29:14–16).

"And **my God** will supply all your needs according to *His riches* in glory in Christ Jesus" (Phil. 4:19).

Whether you earned it in your job or it was given to you, who was the Source of everything that you have?
God.

Principle #4: God wants the first portion of what He gives you.

Many Christians give to their church and other charitable organizations but are not blessed because they don't understand this very important principle. God is clear throughout the entire Bible that He wants to be **first** in every area of your life.

If you pay your bills before returning the *first* back to Him, God is not first in your life and you will have missed the blessing. We learned in chapter 5, "First Love," that God removes from us what we have put ahead of Him.

"Honor the Lord from your wealth, and from the **first** of all your produce; so your barns will be filled with plenty, and your vats will overflow with new wine" (Prov. 3:9). The principle is clear; we **must give to God first.**

Often when Christians begin to consider tithing, they cannot see how they can possibly tithe since they are barely making ends meet. This is because they are also ignorant to what has been happening in their finances. Haggai 1:9 says that God "blows away" what you bring home and He also allows the **devourer** come and take what was rightfully His.

"'Bring the whole tithe into the storehouse, so that there may be food in My house, and test Me now in this,' says the Lord of hosts, 'if I will not open for you the windows of heaven, and pour out for you a blessing until it overflows. *Then* I will **rebuke** the **devourer** for you, so that it may **not destroy** the fruits of the ground; nor will your vine in the field cast its grapes,' says the Lord of hosts" (Mal. 3:10–11).

Every month non-tithing Christians are met with "unexpected" expenses, things like repairs or other needs they did not foresee. But it is only because they are ignorant of this principle. For if God is **first** in your life— first in your heart, first in your day, and first in your finances—then (and only then) will God "open for you the windows of heaven, pour out for you a blessing until it overflows," and faithfully "rebuke the devourer for you."

Those who humble themselves by giving God their tithe and offerings will delight themselves in **abundant** prosperity! "But the *humble* will inherit the land, and will delight themselves in **abundant** *prosperity"* (Ps. 37:11). His Word tells us, "Adversity pursues sinners, but the *righteous* will be **rewarded** with prosperity" (Prov. 13:21).

Principle #5: What you do with the first portion determines what God does with the rest.

When God asked Abraham for His son, he did not withhold him; as a result, God tells him, "for now I know that you fear God, since you have not withheld your son, your only son, from Me. . . . because you have done this thing and have not withheld your son, your only son, indeed I will **greatly bless you** . . ." (Gen. 22:12, 17).

God told the army who took Jericho that they were not to take the spoil of the first city, then God would give them the rest. God always wants to see if we put Him first to test our hearts. "The refining pot is for silver and the furnace for gold, but the Lord tests hearts" (Prov. 17:3). However, one of the soldiers, Akin, could not resist and took some of the spoil. When they were to take the next city, Ai, in a battle that was much smaller and should have easily been won, they were defeated. (See Joshua 6.)

This principle is not just in your finances, or in your restoration, but in every area of your life. When we fail to give to God first, then we are robbing God of what He has asked for. He wants no other gods before Him: not our money, our spouses, our marriages, or our careers. What you do with the first of everything will determine what God will do with the rest—bless it or curse it.

Are you in a financial crisis?

"But seek first His kingdom and His righteousness, and all these things will be added to you" (Matt. 6:33).

Have you sought the Lord about your finances? In Philippians 4:19, the Bible clearly teaches that the Lord is the One who will supply **all** our needs. However, if we go to others with our needs rather than seeking the Lord—if we fail to "seek Him **first**"—then "all these things" will *not* be "added unto" us.

Are you following the principles for financial security in the Lord? The Scriptures teach us that we are to tithe in order to be "filled with plenty" and "overflow" (Prov. 3:9–10). We are also encouraged to "sow" if we want to reap (Gal. 6:7, 2 Cor. 9:6). Have you been sowing and faithfully tithing? Take the time to read these passages of Scripture again and again, then pray for how the Lord wants to change the way that you are trusting Him while fulfilling His command to all believers, beginning by giving a portion back to Him.

If you are tithing faithfully and still in a financial crisis, make sure that you are following all of God's statutes. There are many references in Scripture to actions that lead to poverty, including not asking (James 4:2), asking with wrong motive (James 4:3), adultery (Prov. 6:26), heavy drinking or gluttonous behavior (Prov. 21:17, Prov. 23:21), laziness (Prov. 10:4, Prov. 14:23, Prov. 28:18–20), not accepting rebuke or correction (Prov. 13:18), making hasty decisions (Prov. 21:5), oppressing the poor (Prov. 22:16), living treacherously with your wife (Mal. 2:14–16) or failing to honor her (1 Pet. 3:7) and, of course, withholding from God what is rightfully His.

While we are giving back to God in tithes and offerings, we also need to be sure we are giving our wives the honor they deserve.

"You husbands likewise, live with your wives in an understanding way, as with a weaker vessel, since she is a woman; and *grant her honor* as a fellow heir of the grace of life, so that your prayers may not be hindered" (1 Pet. 3:7). Has your wife been the one who has tried to live within your means but you were irresponsible with your spending? Have you shamed your wife to others or joked about her spending? Be sure you are pure in heart and faithful to your wife in every way.

When Erin was in financial ruin as a single mother of four young children, she learned the principle of tithing. Even though she lived close to poverty level, she began tithing for the first time in her life (being raised as a Catholic she had never even heard of the principle). Not only did she sow by tithing ten percent of the meager amount of the money she received, but she also sowed into the lives of women who were experiencing tragedy in their lives (telling them about God's ability to restore their marriages).

Erin's obedient heart that learned to tithe to the Lord set the standard in our home when I was gone. God honored her by leading me to tithe soon after I came home without her even telling me!

Men, if you are still struggling with giving, it may help you to know that God owns everything we have, and it is only because of Him that we have been given the "power to make wealth, that He may confirm His covenant" with us. (Deut. 8:18). Therefore you need to make sure that you give to Him **first** to confirm that He is **first** in your life!

Will you serve God or mammon (money)?

Too many shy away from teaching on giving because of the abuses and because they don't want to be considered "money seekers," but it doesn't eliminate the truth in the message. Search for the truth yourself. Test Him to see if He is faithful to His promise. Give to God first, tithe to your storehouse (where you are spiritually fed), and see if your life changes and you are blessed in all areas of your life.

God is the one who provides for our ministry and for our family. We sow into the lives of those who are brokenhearted and water with ongoing support through our fellowship, but it is God who brings the increase. We look to no one to supply our needs but God alone.

Failing to properly teach such an important principle would be to neglect to feed the sheep and shepherd those who are coming to us for help, support, and direction.

Jesus said to feed His sheep, and God said in Hosea that His people perished for a lack of knowledge (Hos. 4:6). Many who come to us are new Christians or have been attending a church where this principle, and other principles of restoration, are not taught. Our job is to make disciples of the Lord, to give them the tools they need to transform their lives.

For those of you who have never given God His tithe, may God prove to you that you can do more with 90% of your income than the 100% than you used to control. It will take a step of faith, but, just like when you chose to restore your marriage rather than moving on, your life will never be the same.

For those of you who do give (but God is not first), may you rearrange your priorities in every area of your life to show God that He has first place.

God is a God who longs to be gracious to us; He longs to bless us! ". . . And let them say continually, "the Lord be magnified, **who delights in the prosperity of His servant"** (Ps. 35:27).

Let me close with this wonderful **promise:** "Those who **sow** in tears shall **reap** with joyful shouting" (Ps. 126:5). **Hallelujah!!**

Personal commitment: to give. "Based on what I have learned in Scripture, I commit to trusting and blessing the Lord with my finances. I will seek the Lord regarding how and where to tithe. I will sow into restoring marriages through sharing the good news about restoration with those whom God brings into my life and through my giving financially as God leads and faithfully provides for me."

Date: _____ Signed: _____

About the Author

Erin Thiele has been blessed to be the mother of seven: four boys, Dallas, Axel, Easton, and Cooper, and three girls, Tyler, Tara, and Macy. Erin's restoration journey began in 1989 when her husband left her for another woman, eventually divorcing her!

In her desperation as a single mother of four small children, Erin searched for help. All the "experts" and numerous pastors from many denominations said the same thing and did their best to convince Erin that her marriage was hopeless—but then, her life changed forever.

Erin found the Mighty Counselor and many PROMISES from Him in His Word. While reading her husband's Bible (that he left behind) she came across ONE verse that changed her life and began her ministry of helping other women:

"For nothing will be impossible with God." Luke 1:37

To Erin this meant, nothing, NOT ONE THING, was impossible WITH God. If a man who didn't want her and who said he didn't love her, could *not* possibly return, then she believed that God would have said so!

This began Erin's intense study in God's Word, the Bible, where she found hundreds MORE of His promises. Each promise increased her faith in the Lord to restore her marriage. And that's when she told God, "If you do this for me [restore my marriage] then I will spend the rest of my life telling the world that nothing, NOT ONE THING, is impossible with You."

Erin's two-year journey took her through the "valley of the shadow of death." After her husband's disappearance, and discovering that her house had been cleared out while visiting her parents in Florida, her husband suddenly showed up three months later.

Erin's trials then increased when her husband moved his girlfriend in with him, close by, in order to spend more time with his children. Each night, Erin's husband walked out on her, leaving again and again, going back to his apartment to sleep with the other woman.

Yet, through everything—being left alone as a single mother of four very young children, with no financial support, AND while everyone was telling her she was crazy to believe God would restore her marriage—she continued to believe.

Then, just as Erin had said, everyone else was wrong and He was right—nothing was impossible with Him! Just two years after her husband left, he returned and their marriage was restored!!

Erin's willingness to trust God and travel *through* the valley of the shadow of death with Him resulted in God blessing her beyond anything anyone could ever have imagined. This journey led Erin to become an author, a minister, AND even more wonderful, Erin was blessed with three more restoration babies (as her husband would call them), her three youngest children.

Erin has written many other books with her distinctive style of using the Scriptures to minister to the brokenhearted and the spiritual captives. Through Erin's books and ministry she has helped countless women (and even men on their own website) restore their marriages—just as God restored hers—"He sent **His Word** and healed them, and delivered them from all their destructions" (Ps. 107:20).

Our ministry has many more resources for women (and men) to help you no matter what crisis you're in. To find all of Erin's books, please visit:

www.RMIEW.com

And, if you want to see God move in *your* life and marriage, come to our website and consider becoming a member of Restoration Fellowship.

Restore Ministries International

POB 830

Ozark, MO 65721

USA

For more help
please visit us at:

EncouragingMen.net

RMIEW.com

Made in the USA
San Bernardino, CA
27 February 2017